Images in this Book

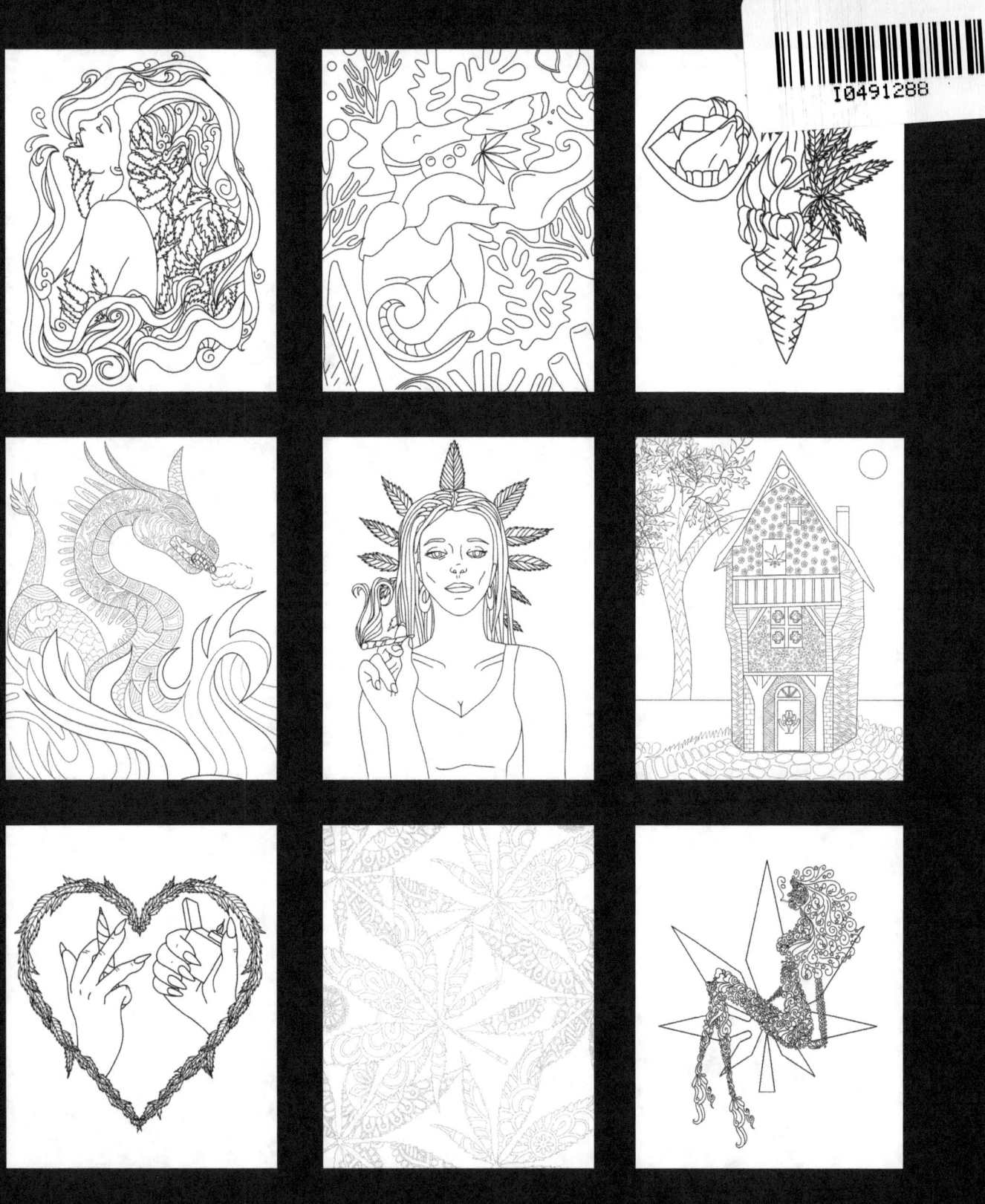

and much more!

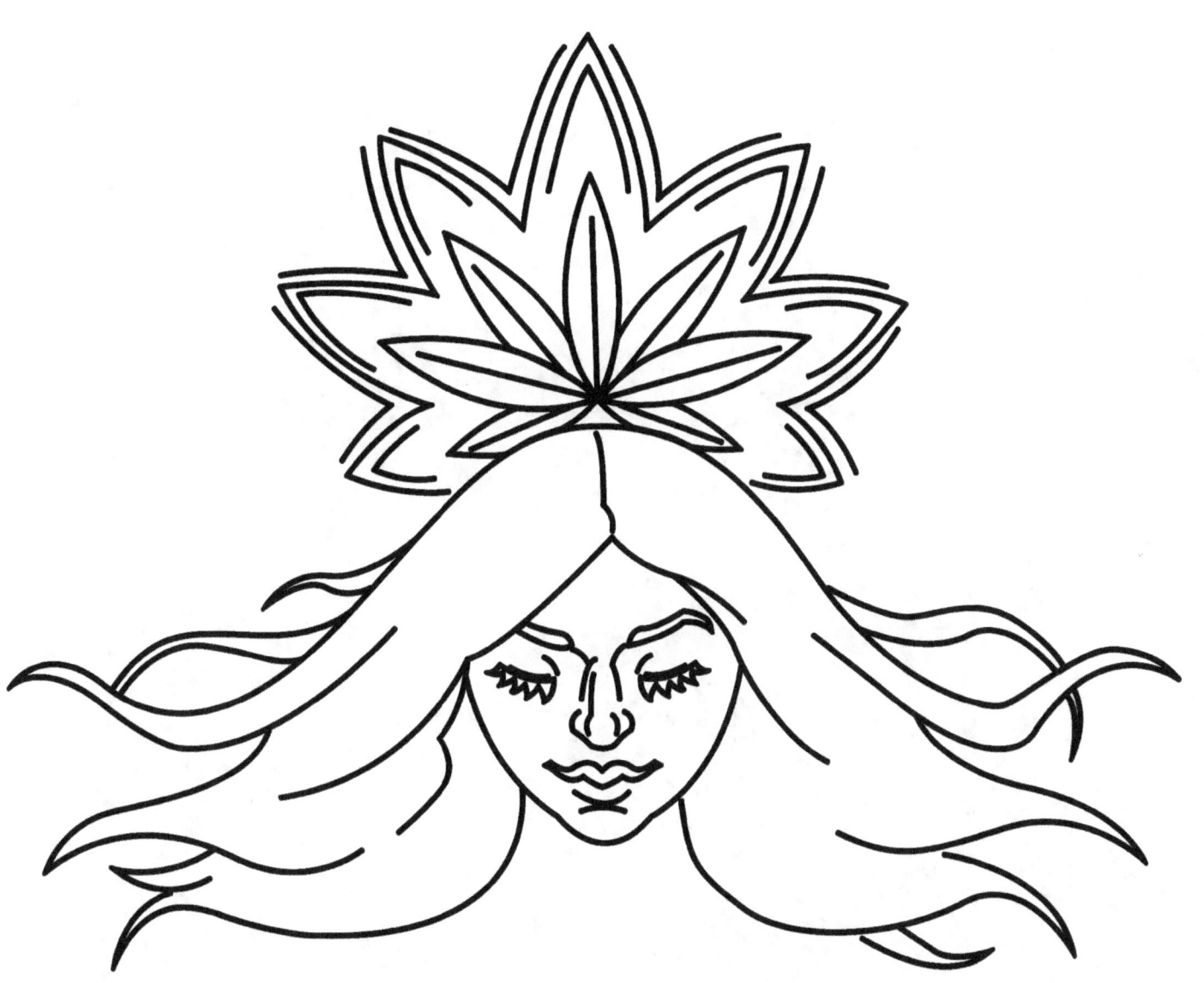

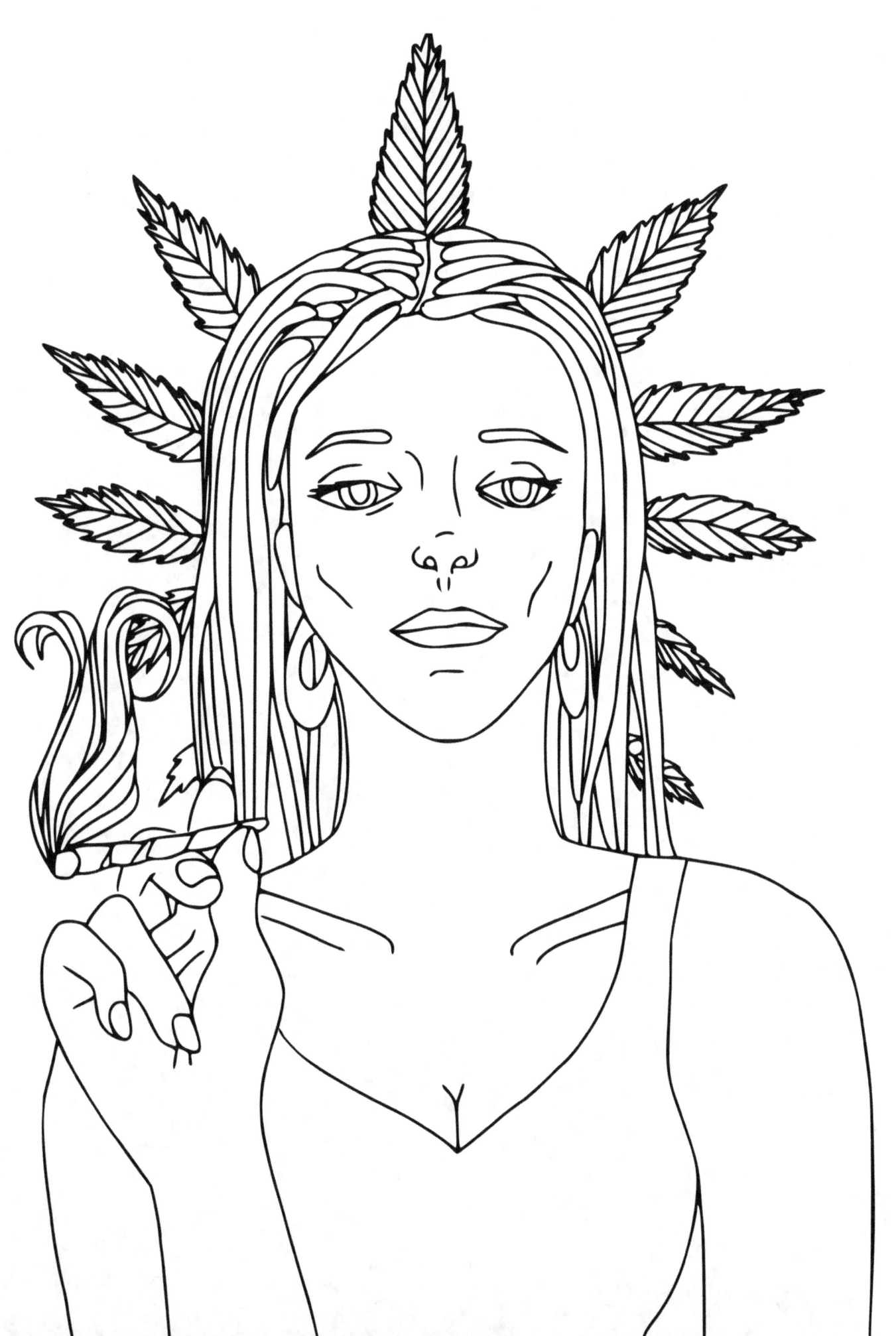

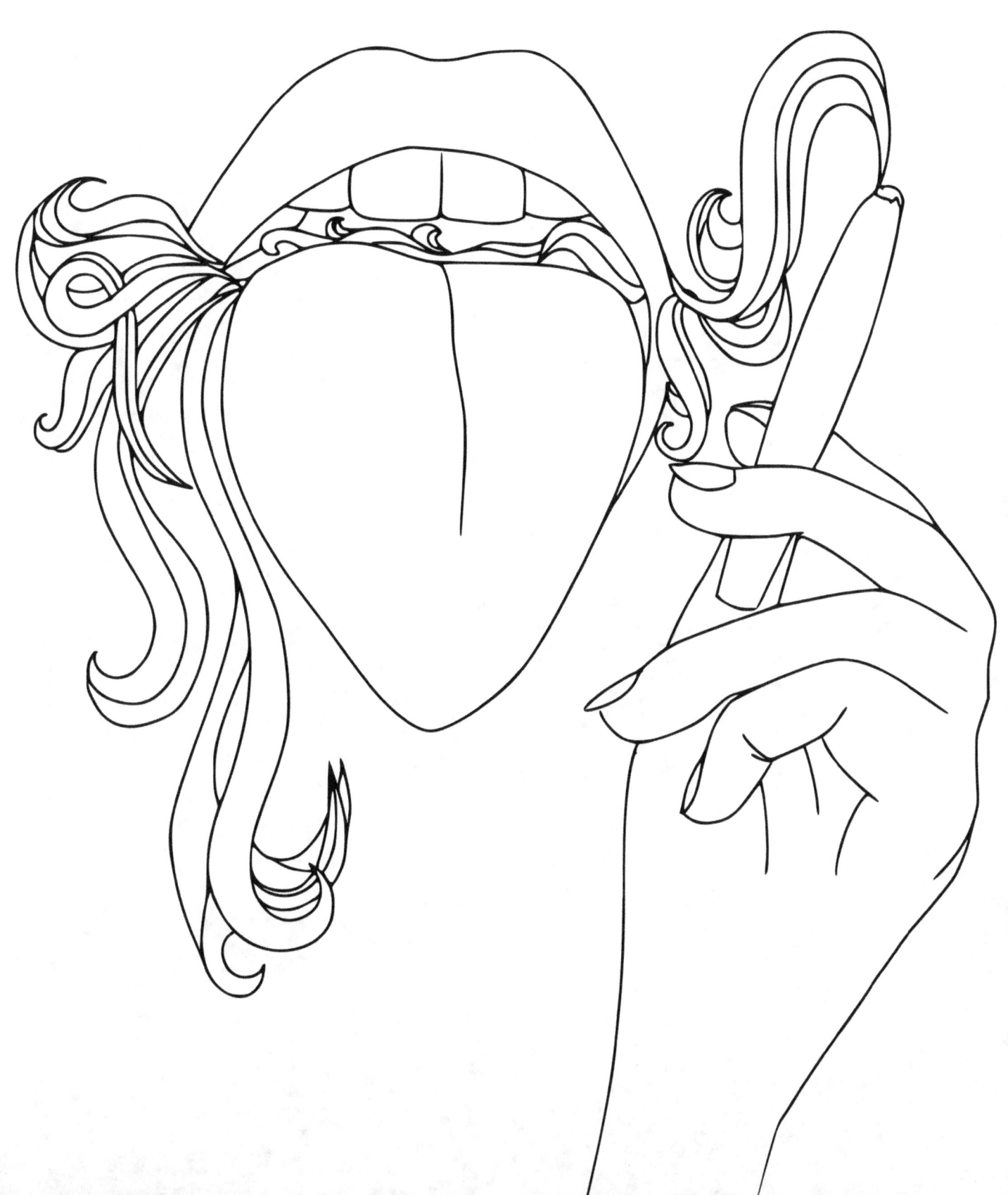

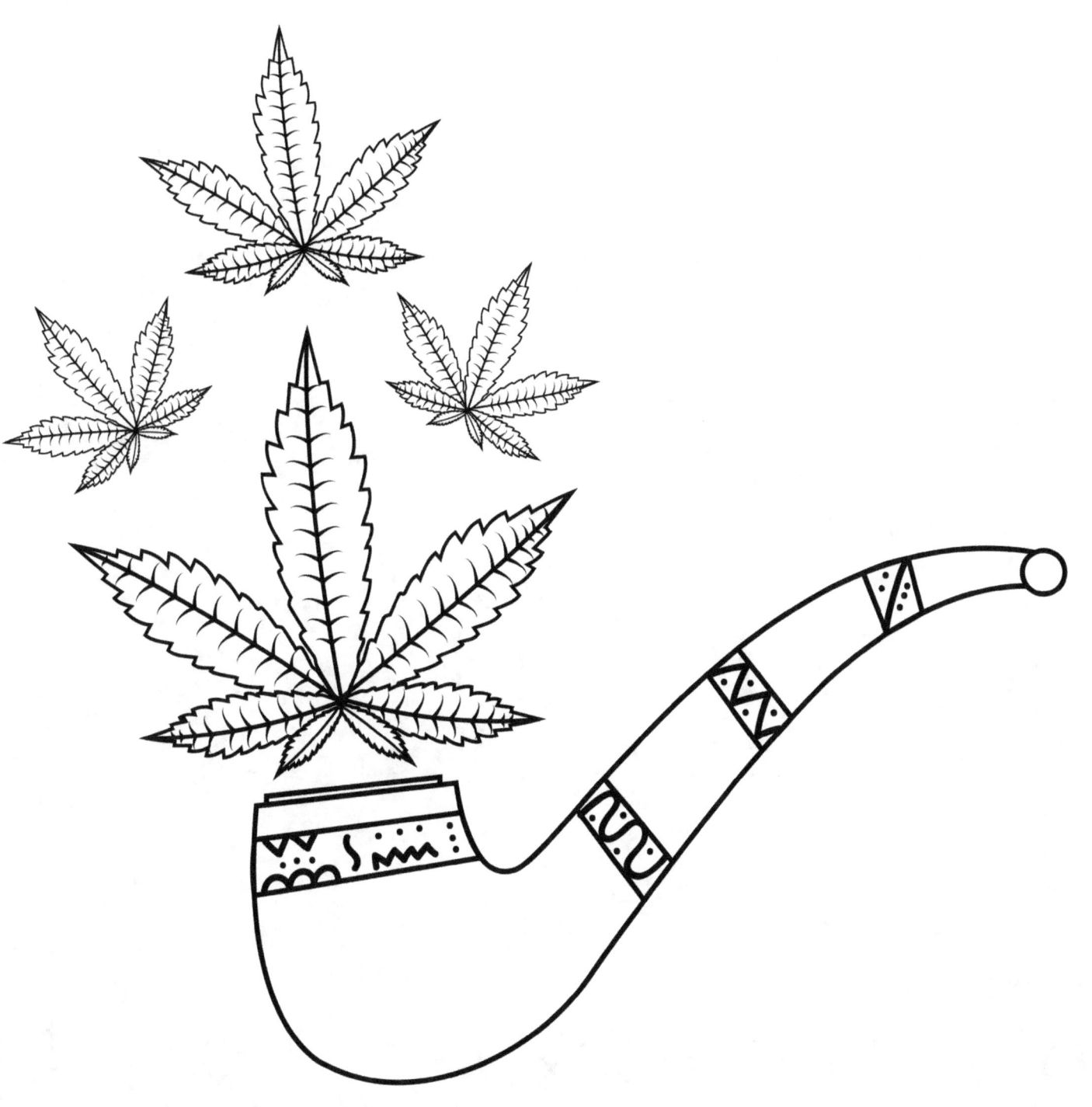

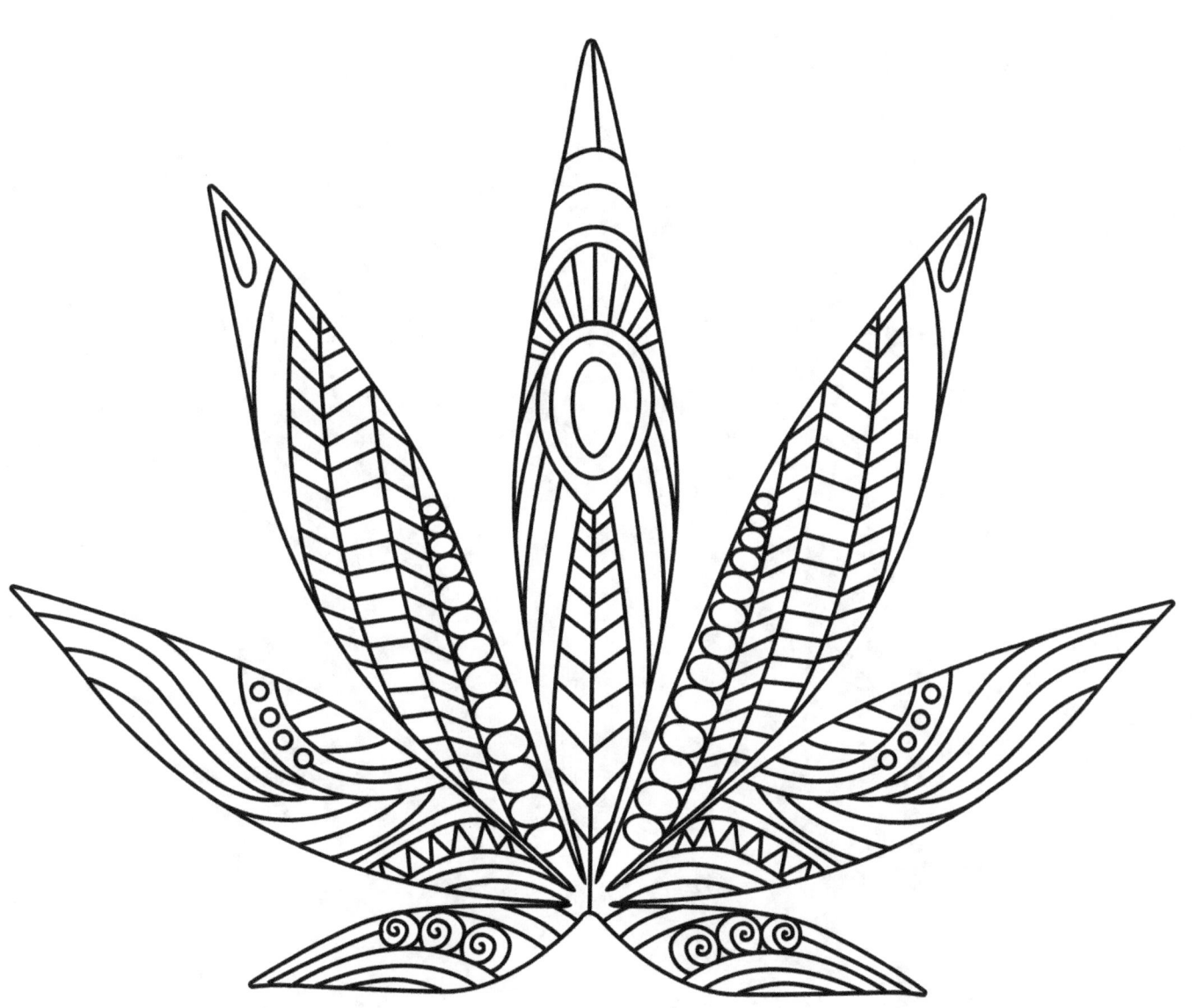

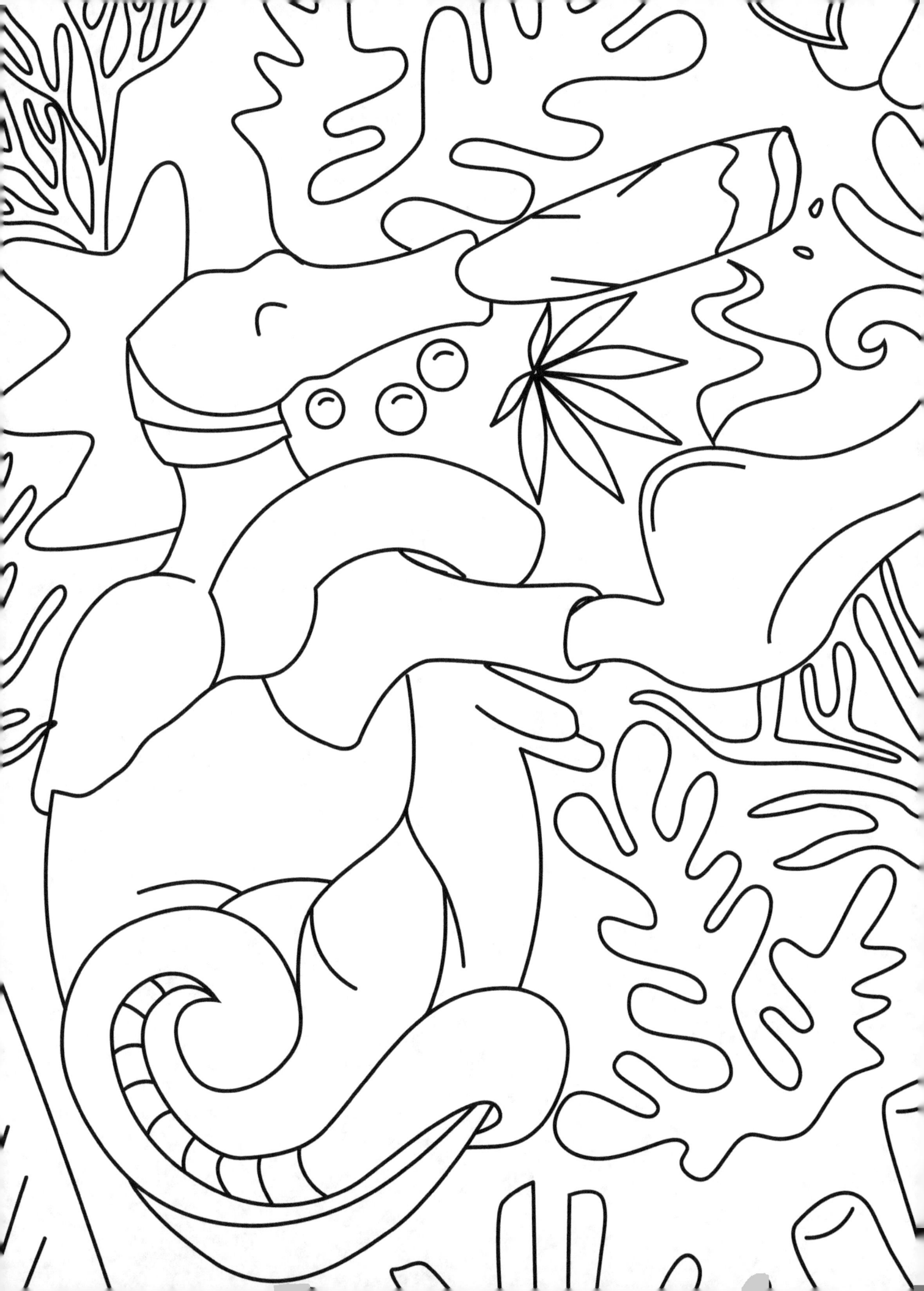

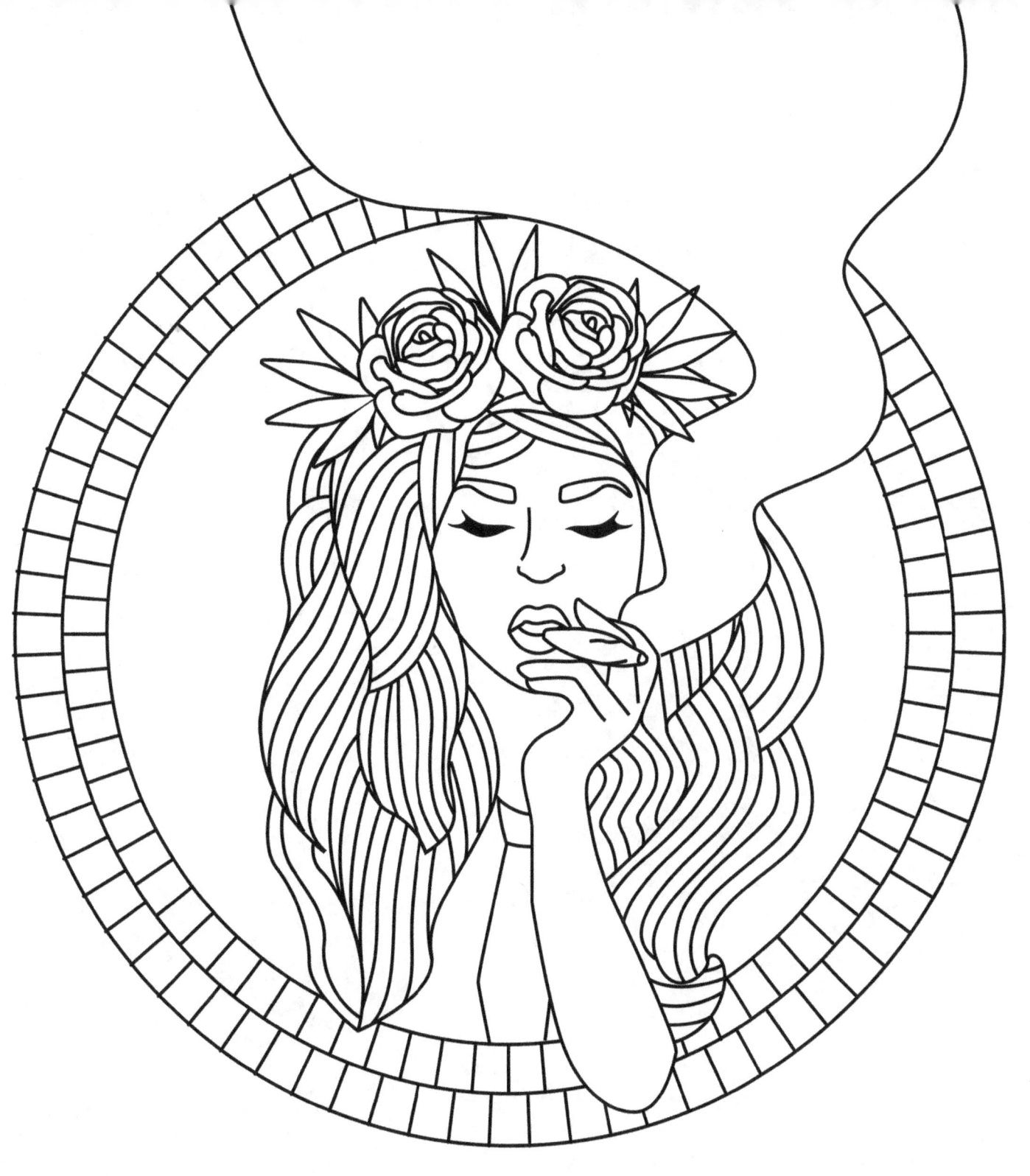

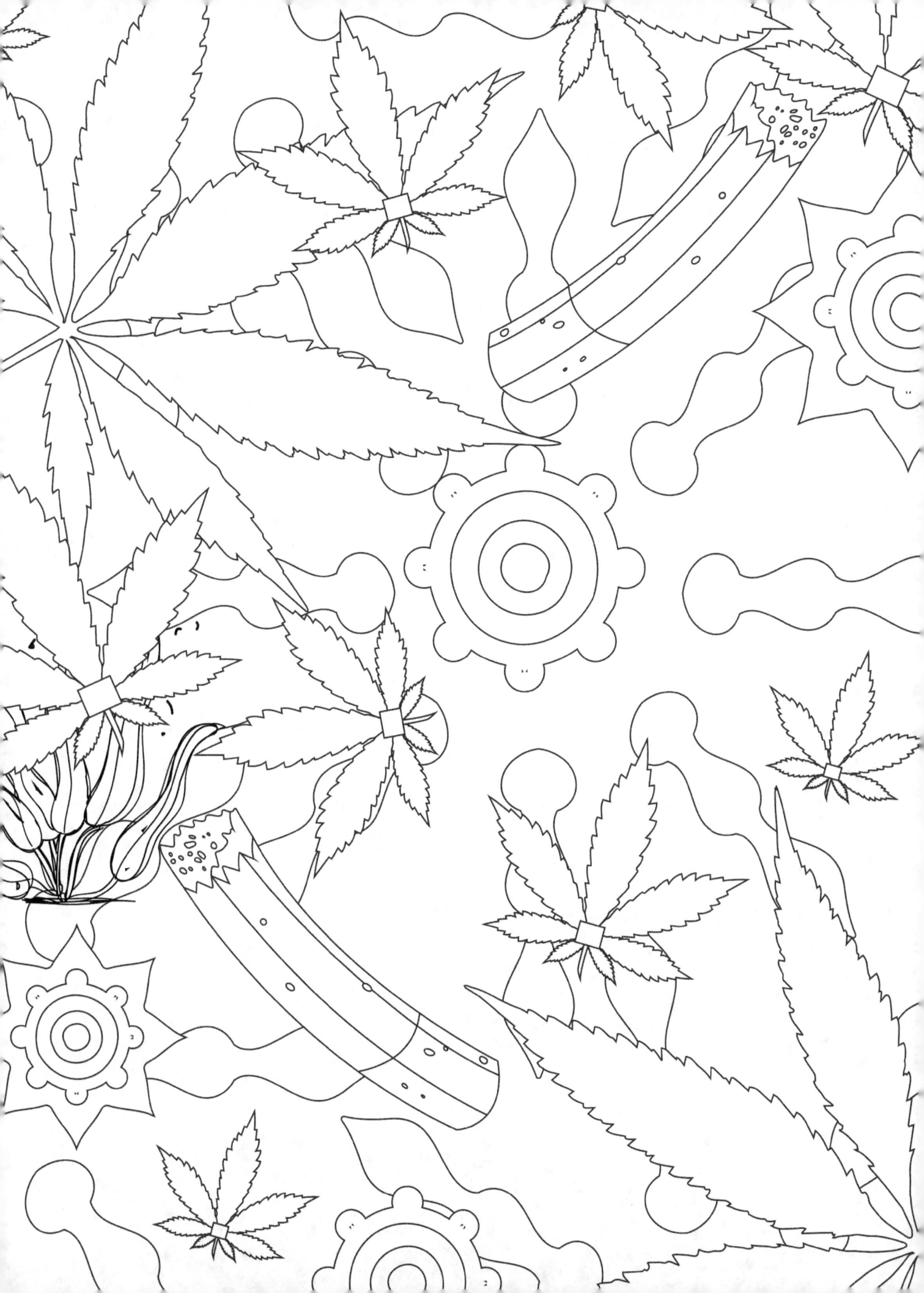

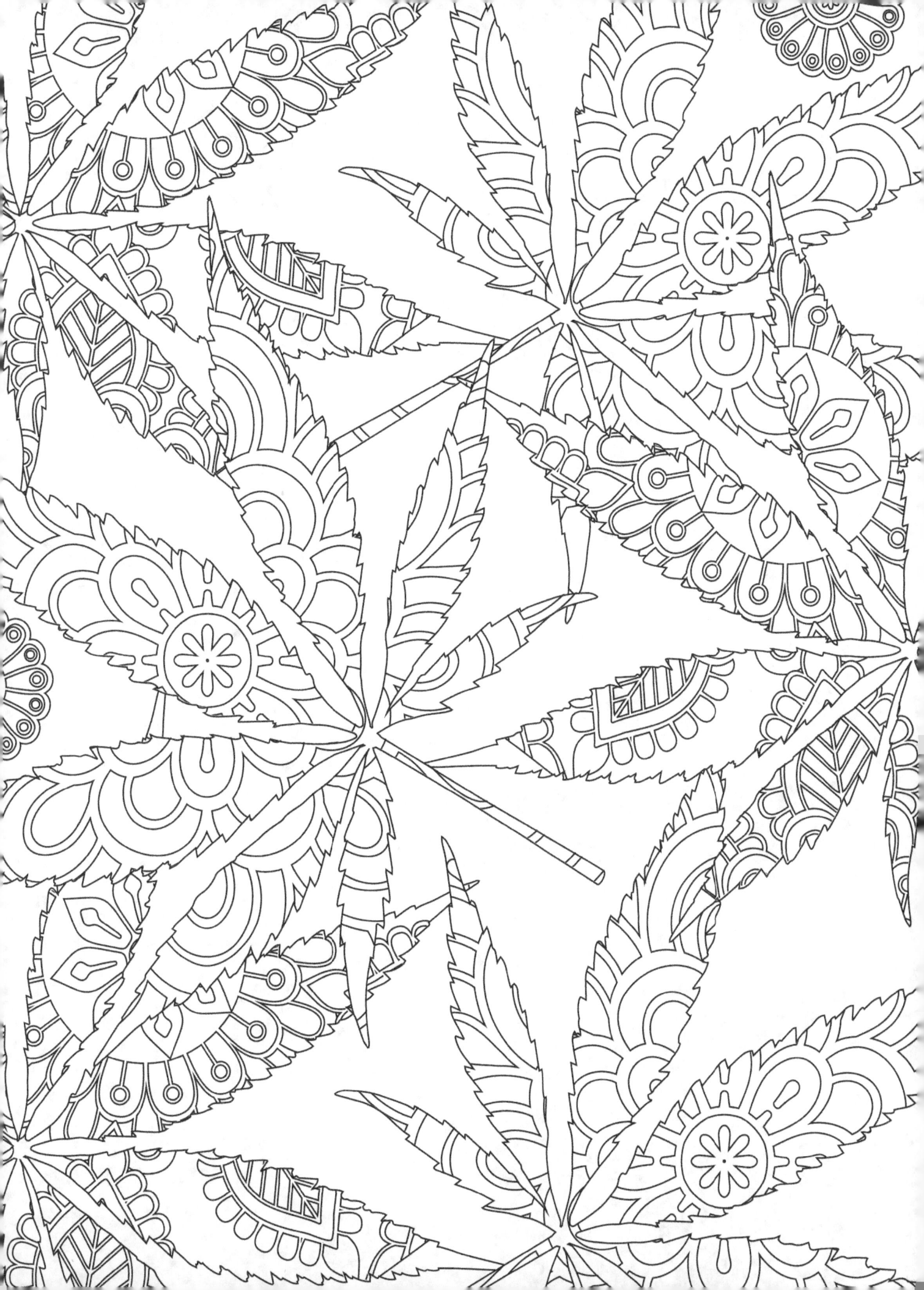

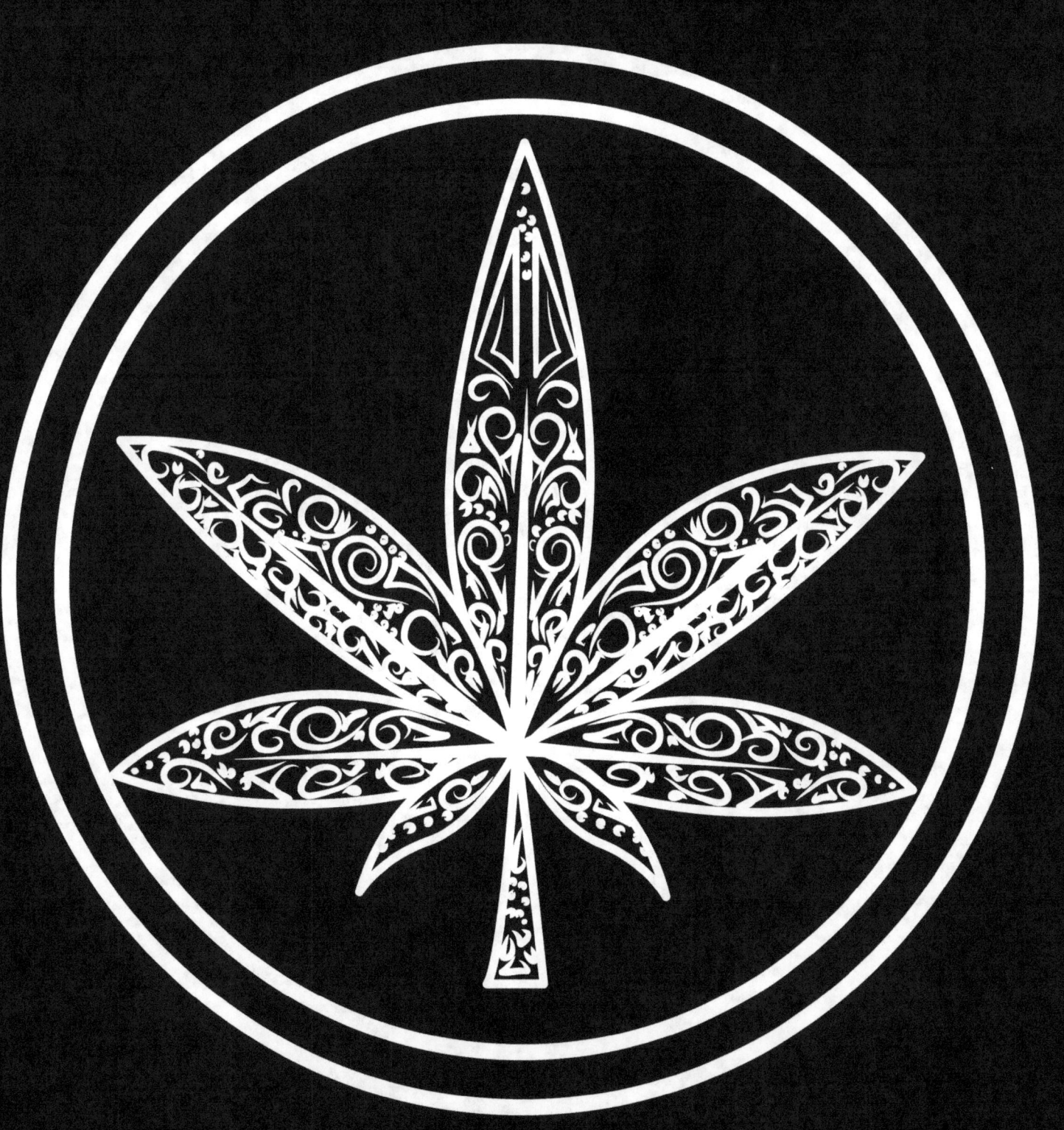

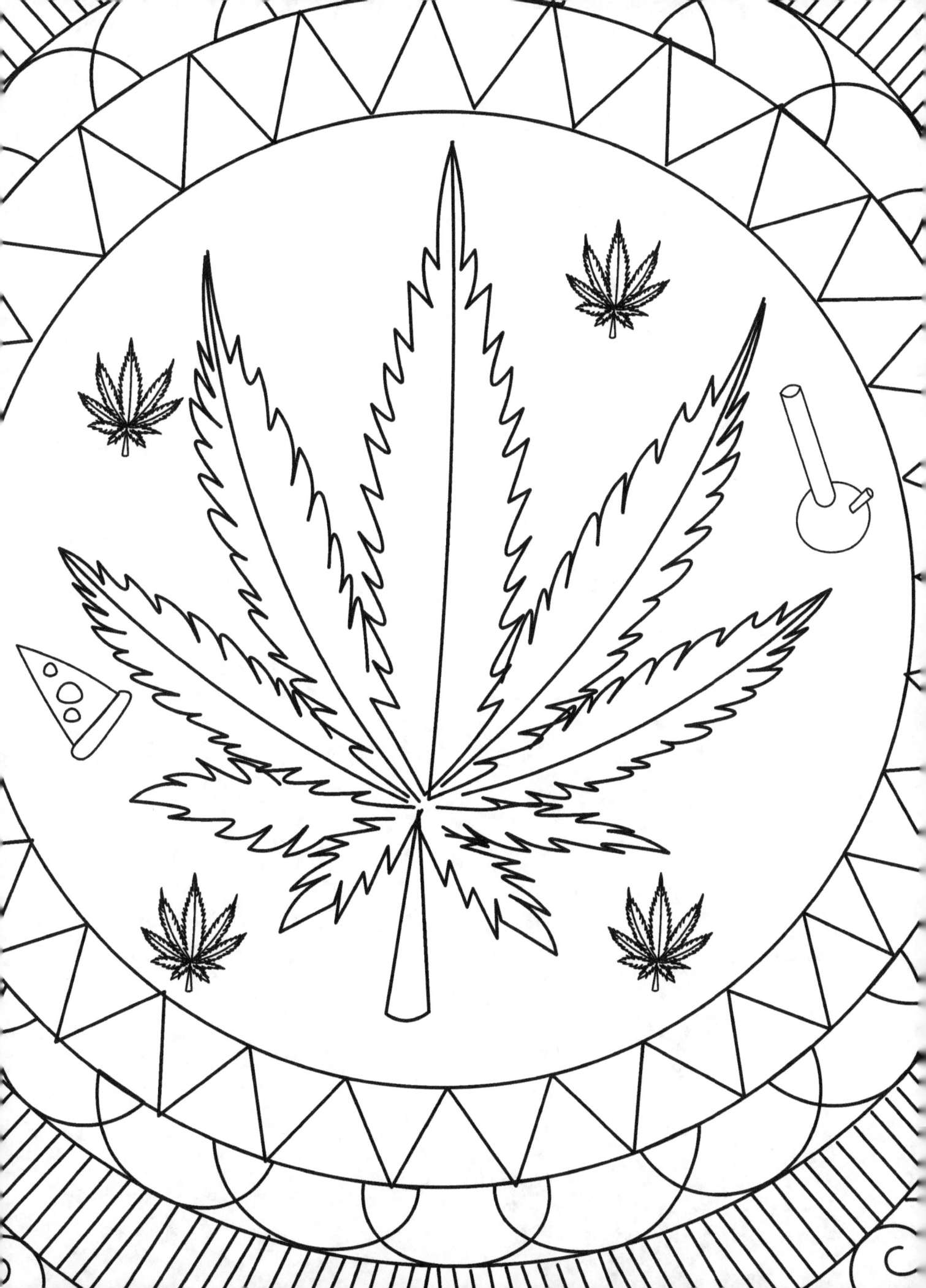

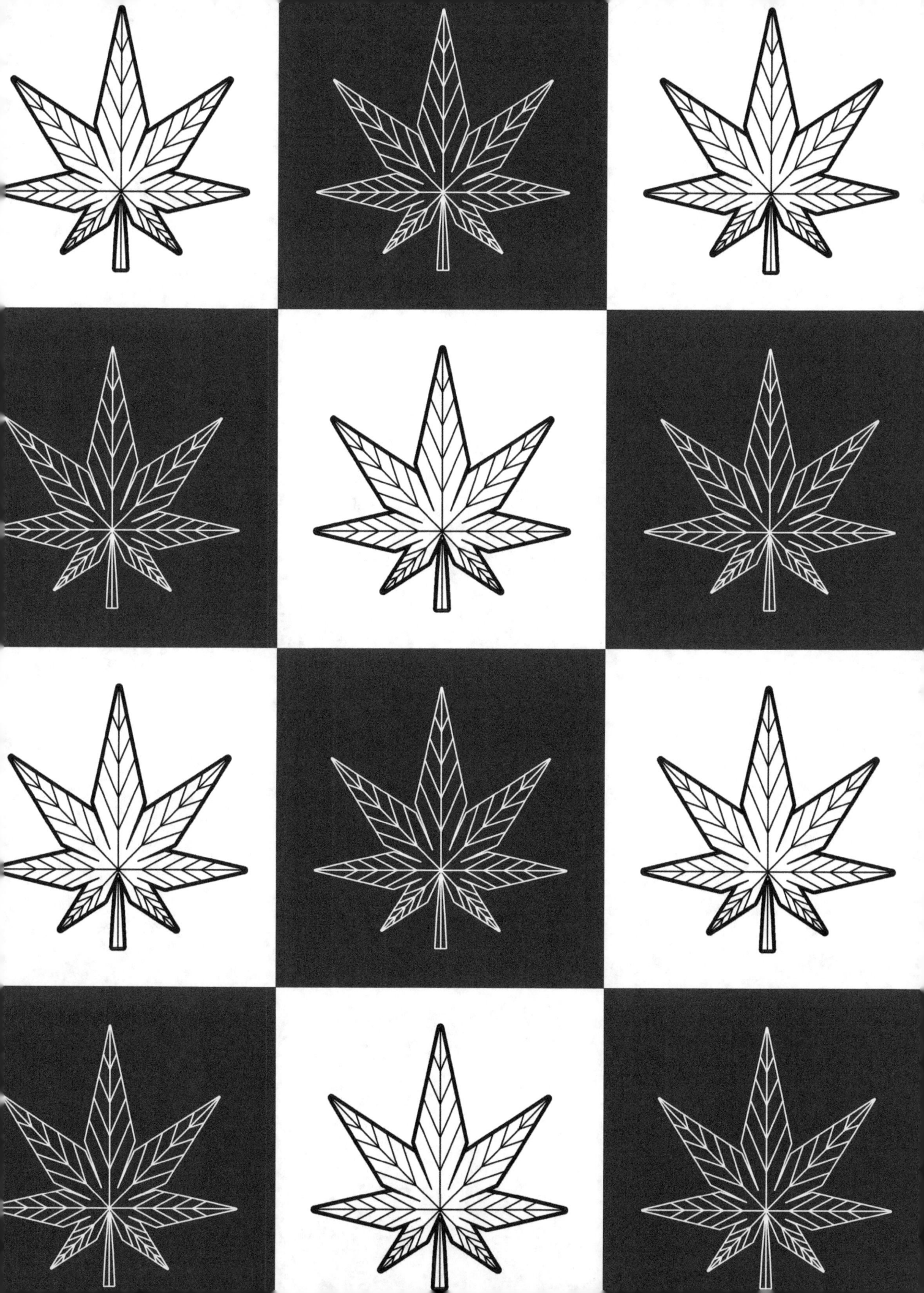

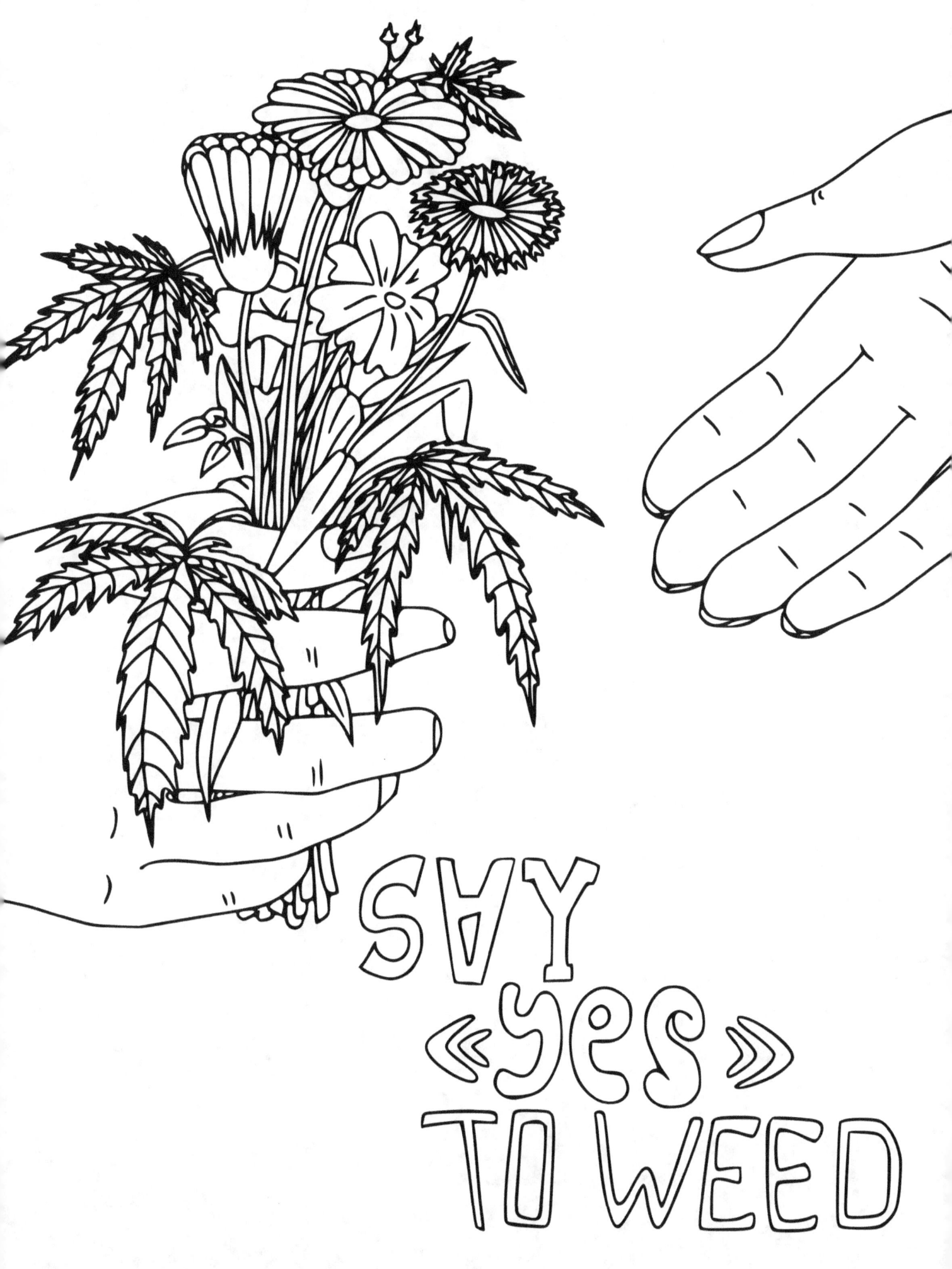

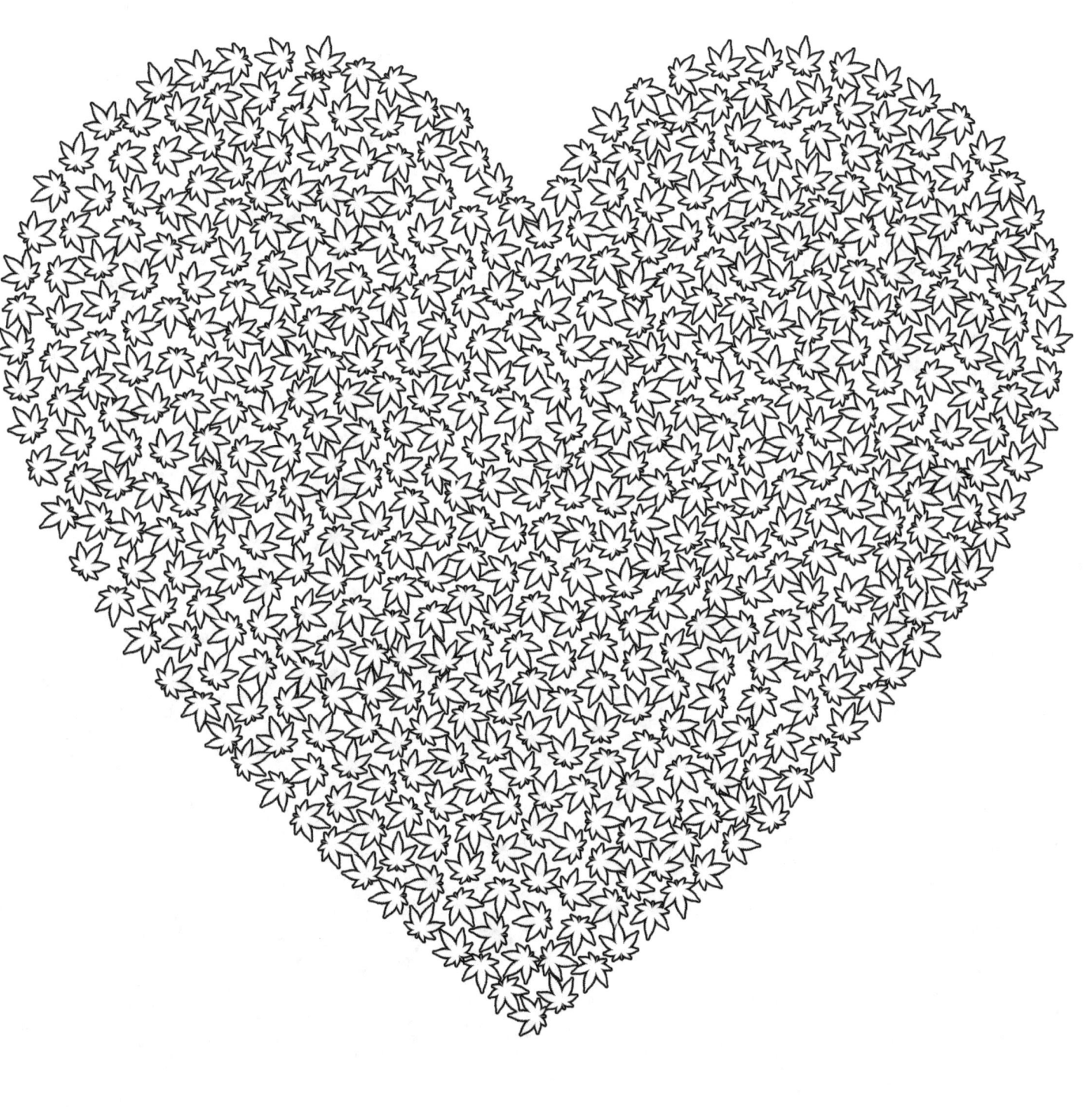

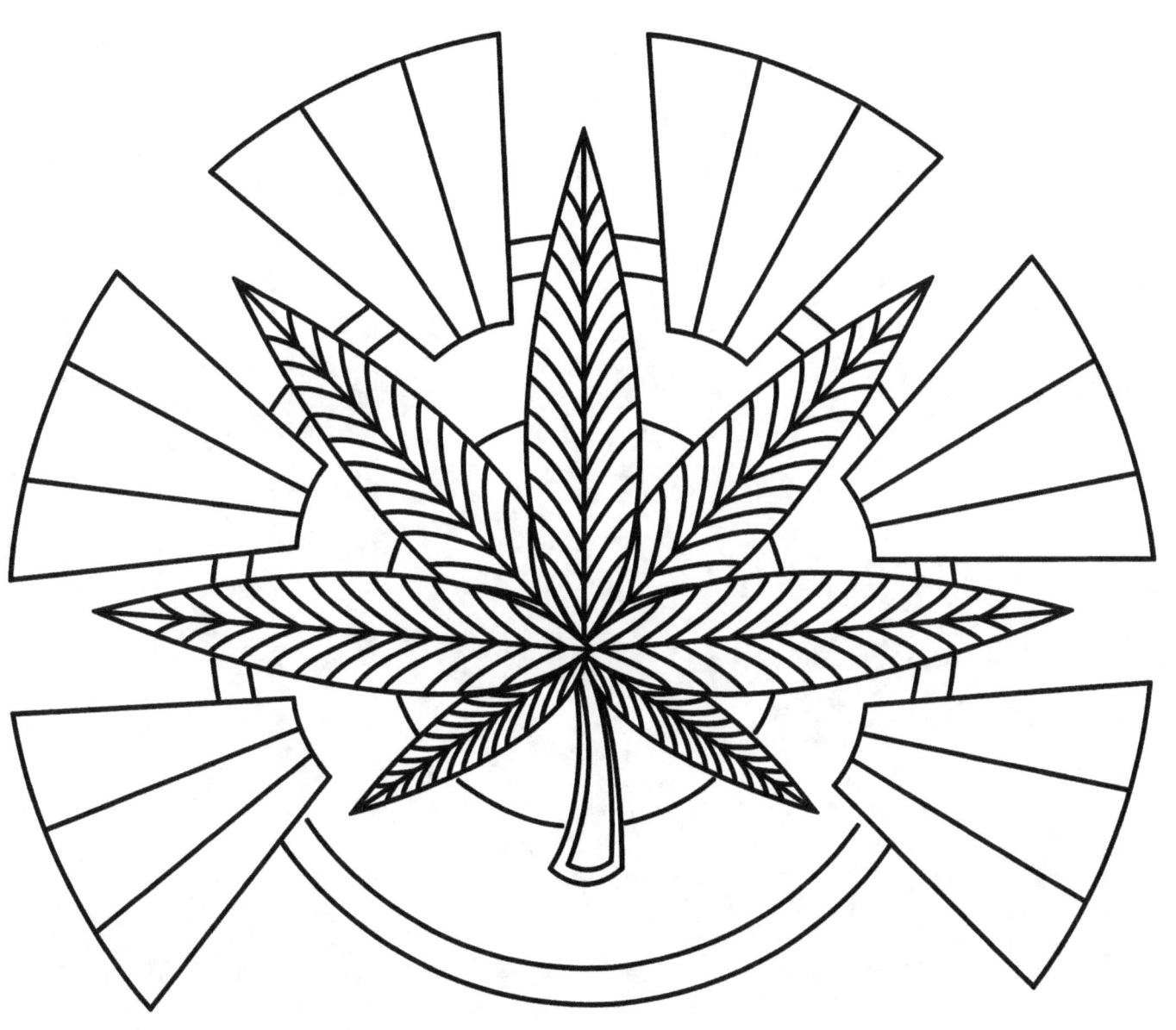

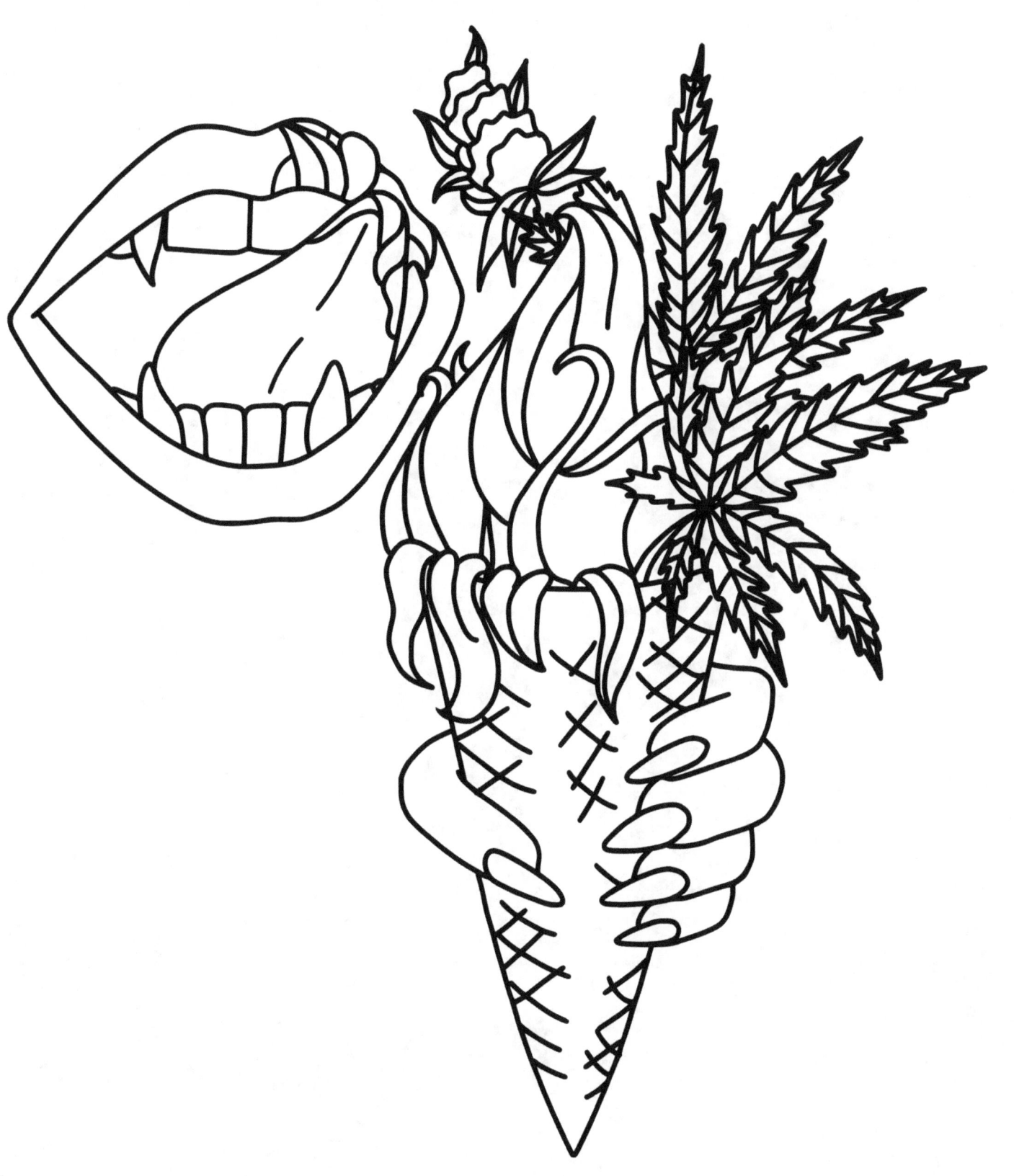

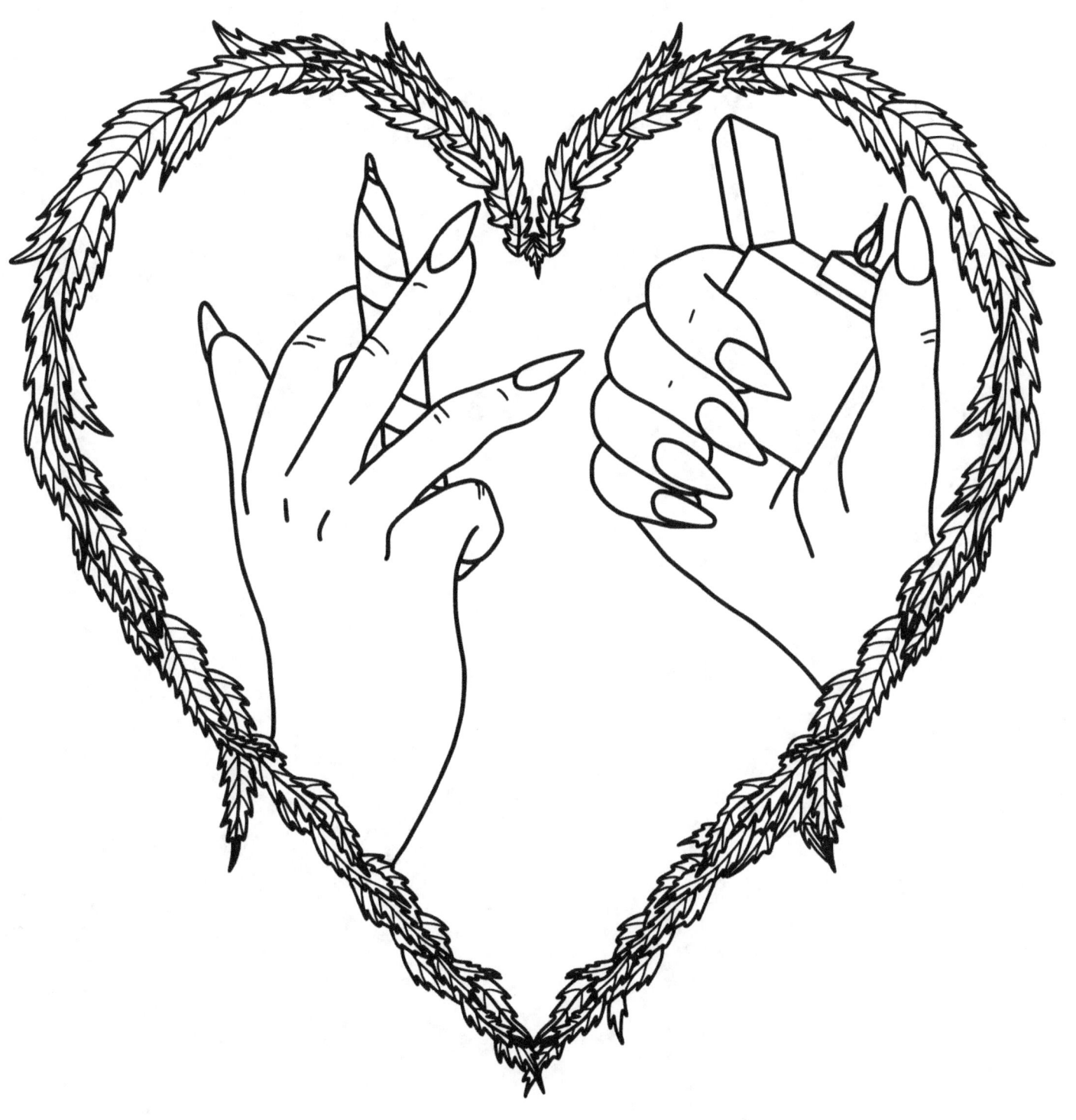

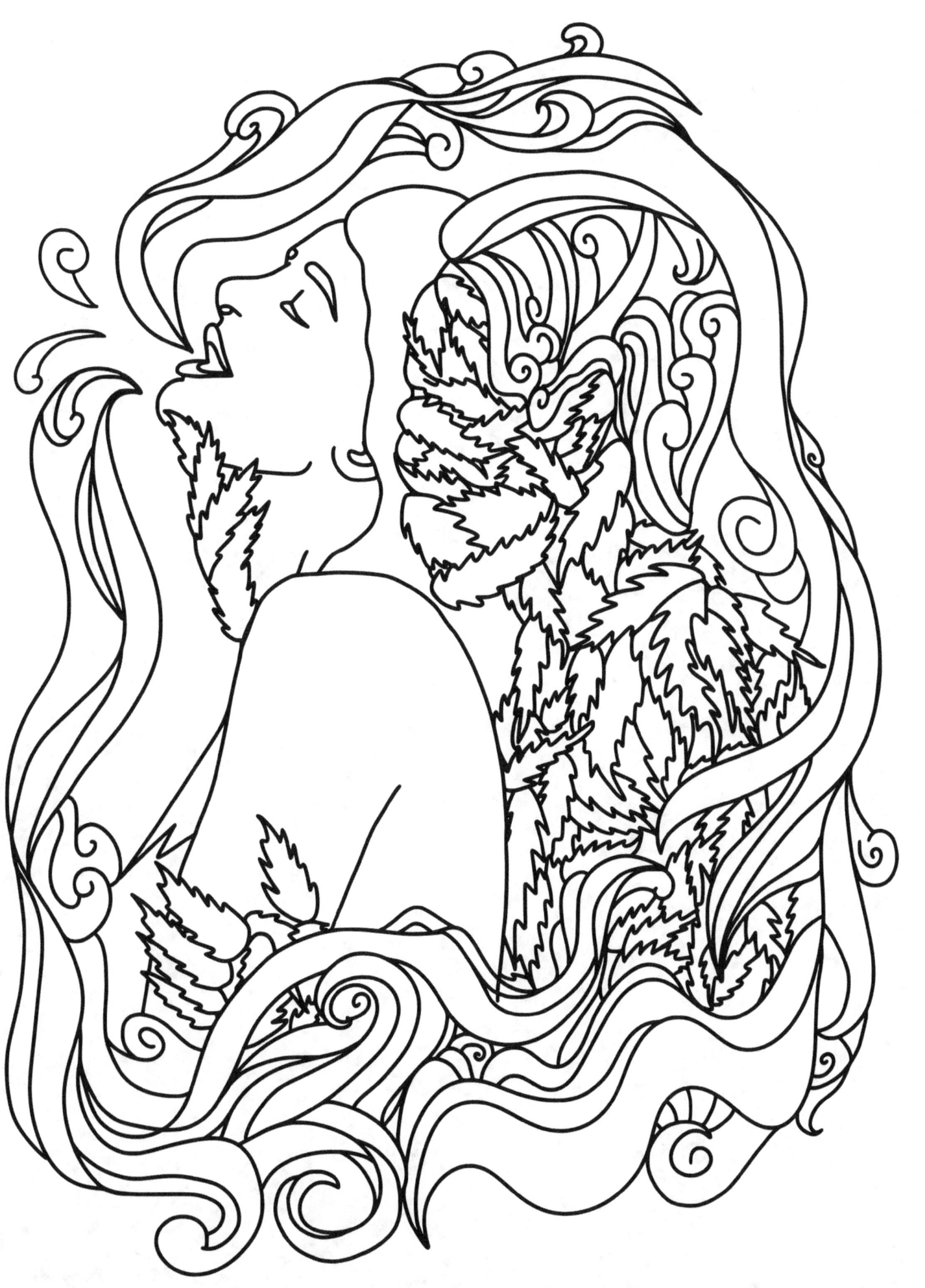

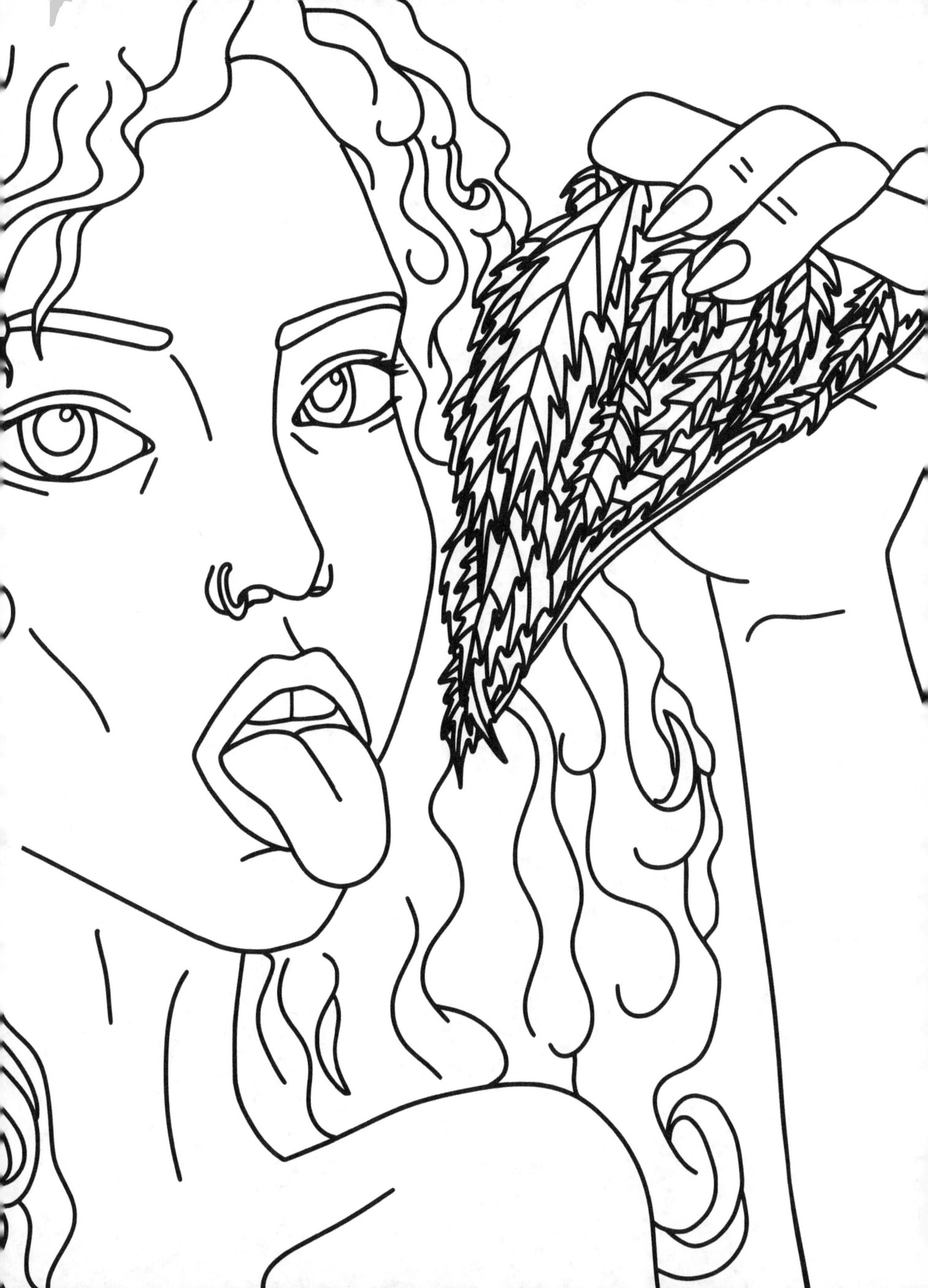

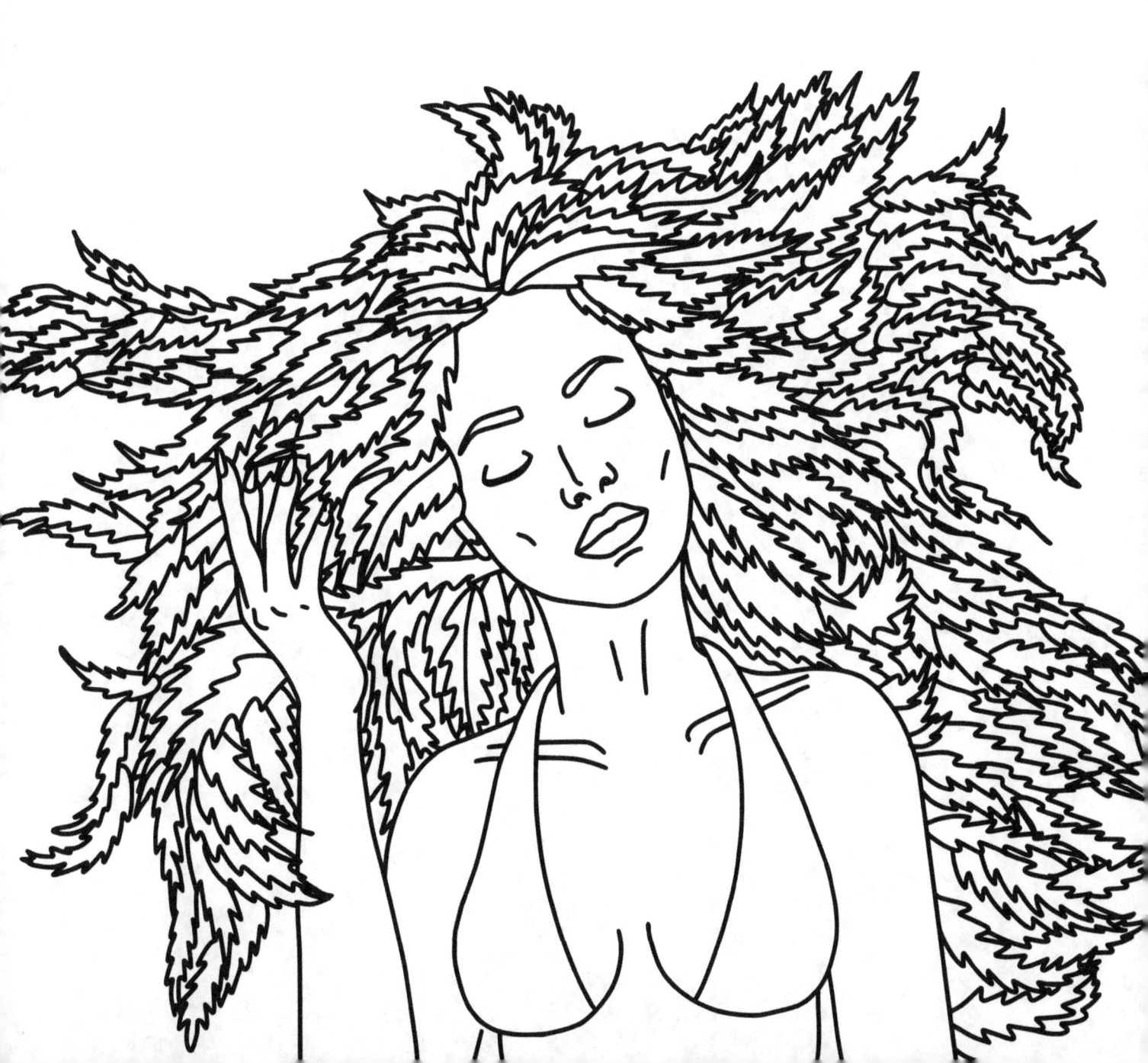

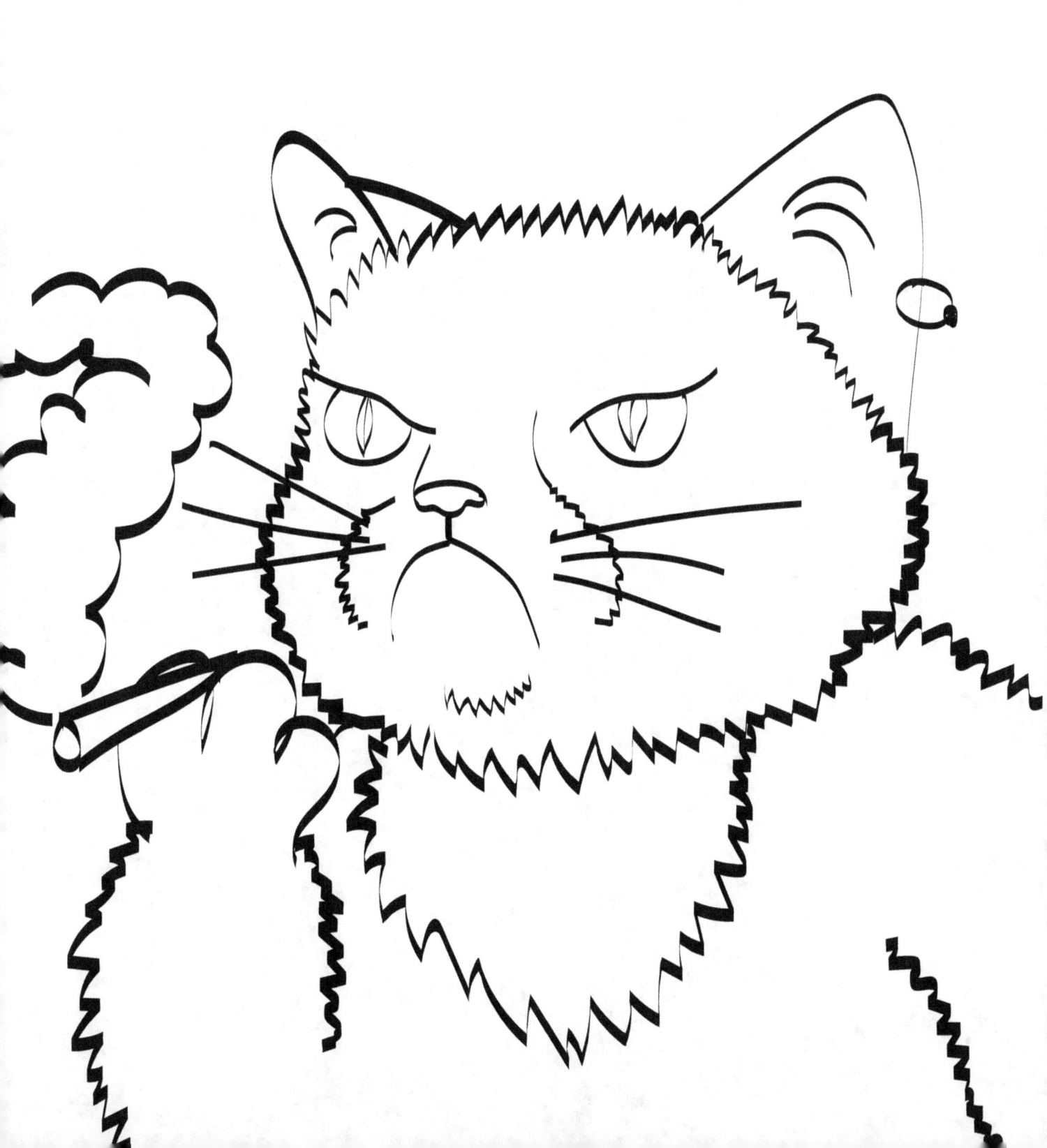

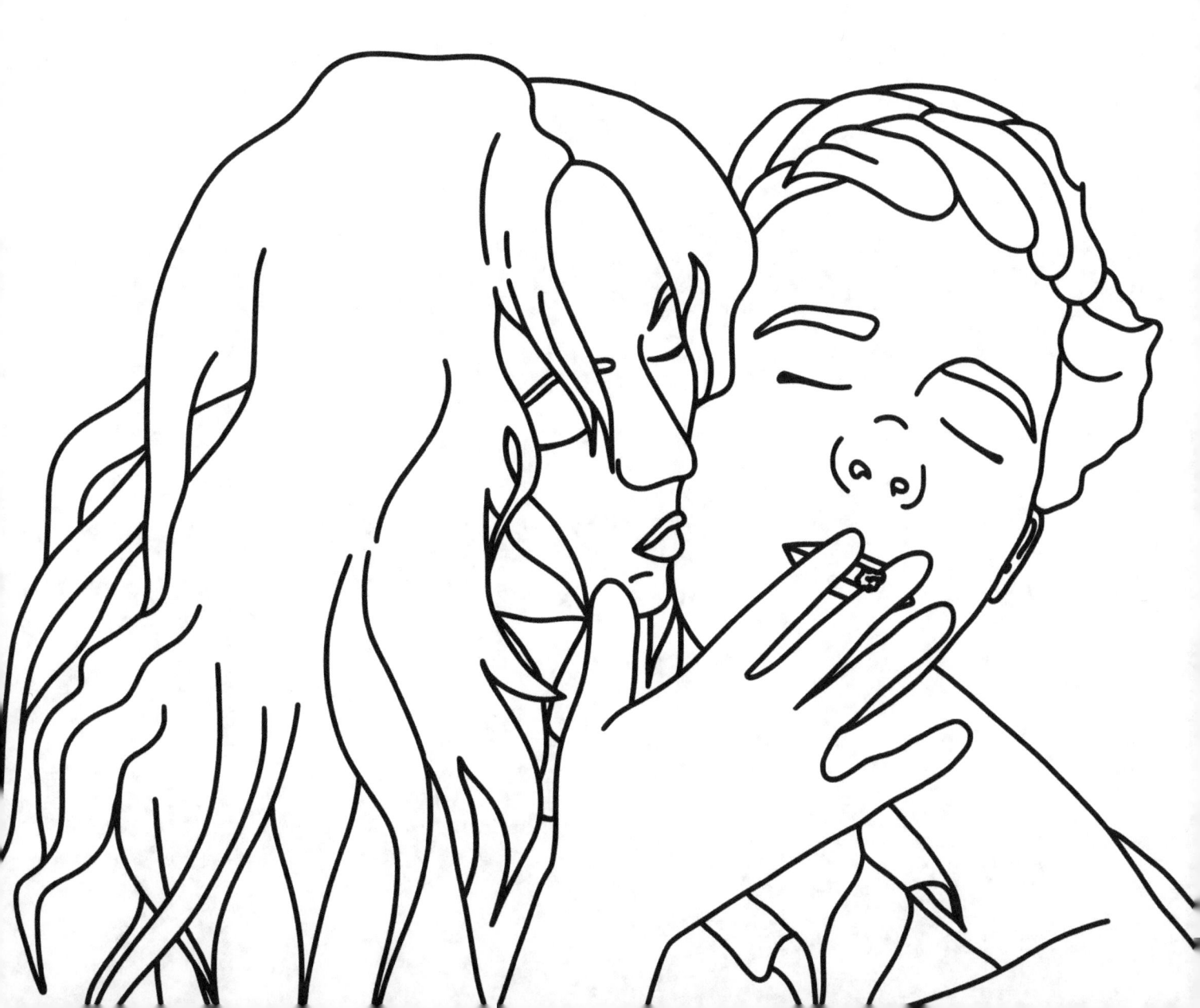

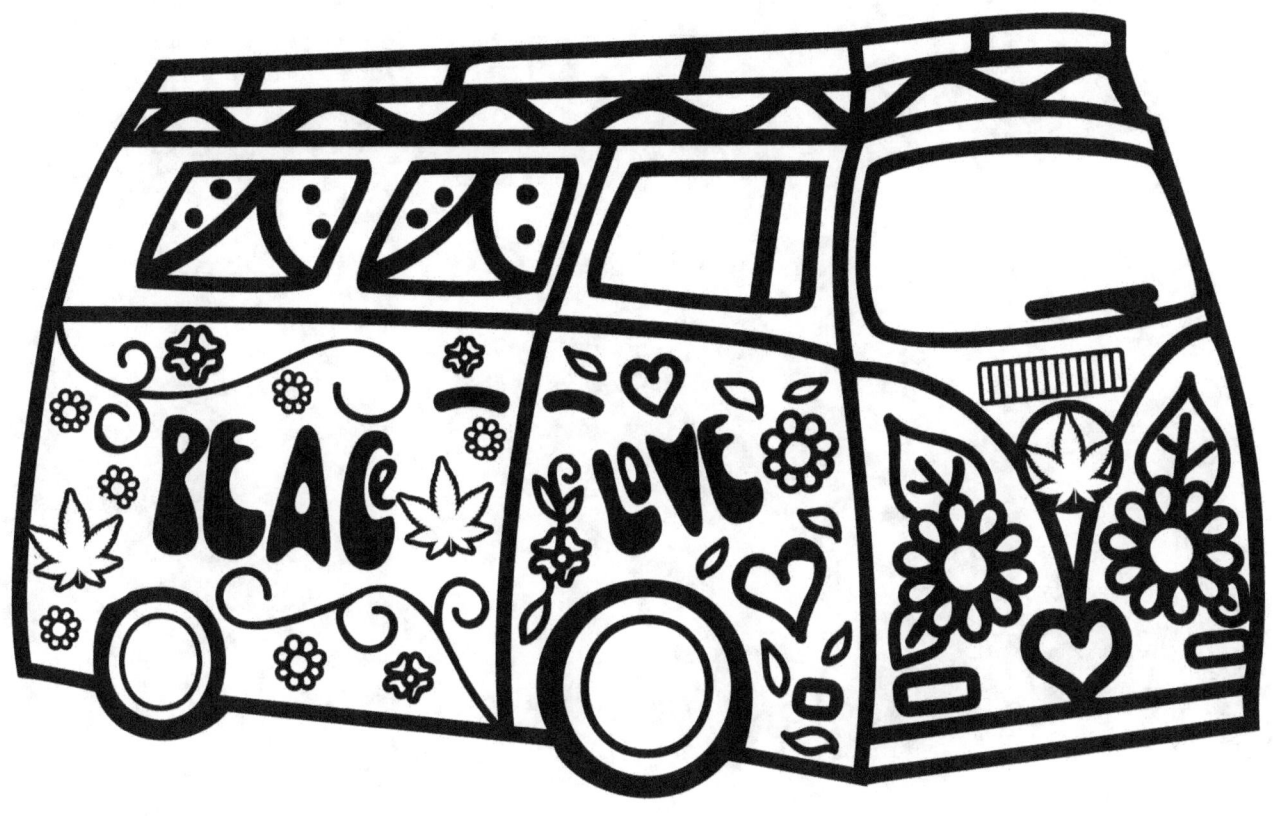

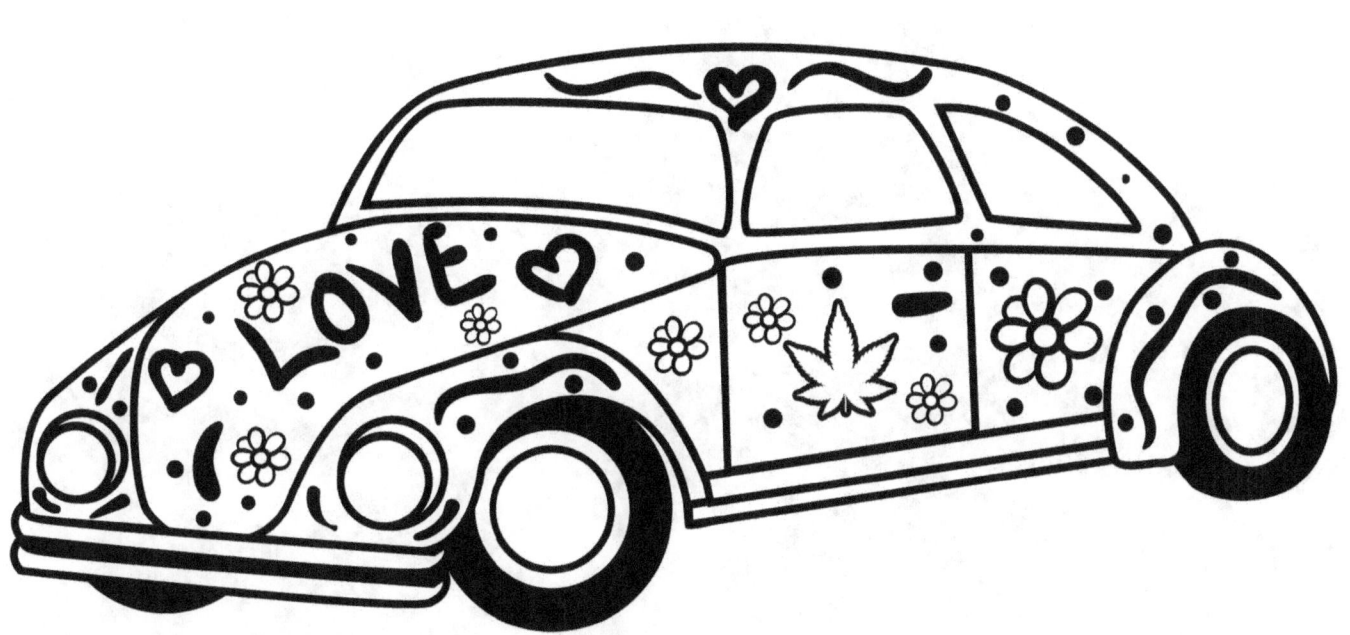

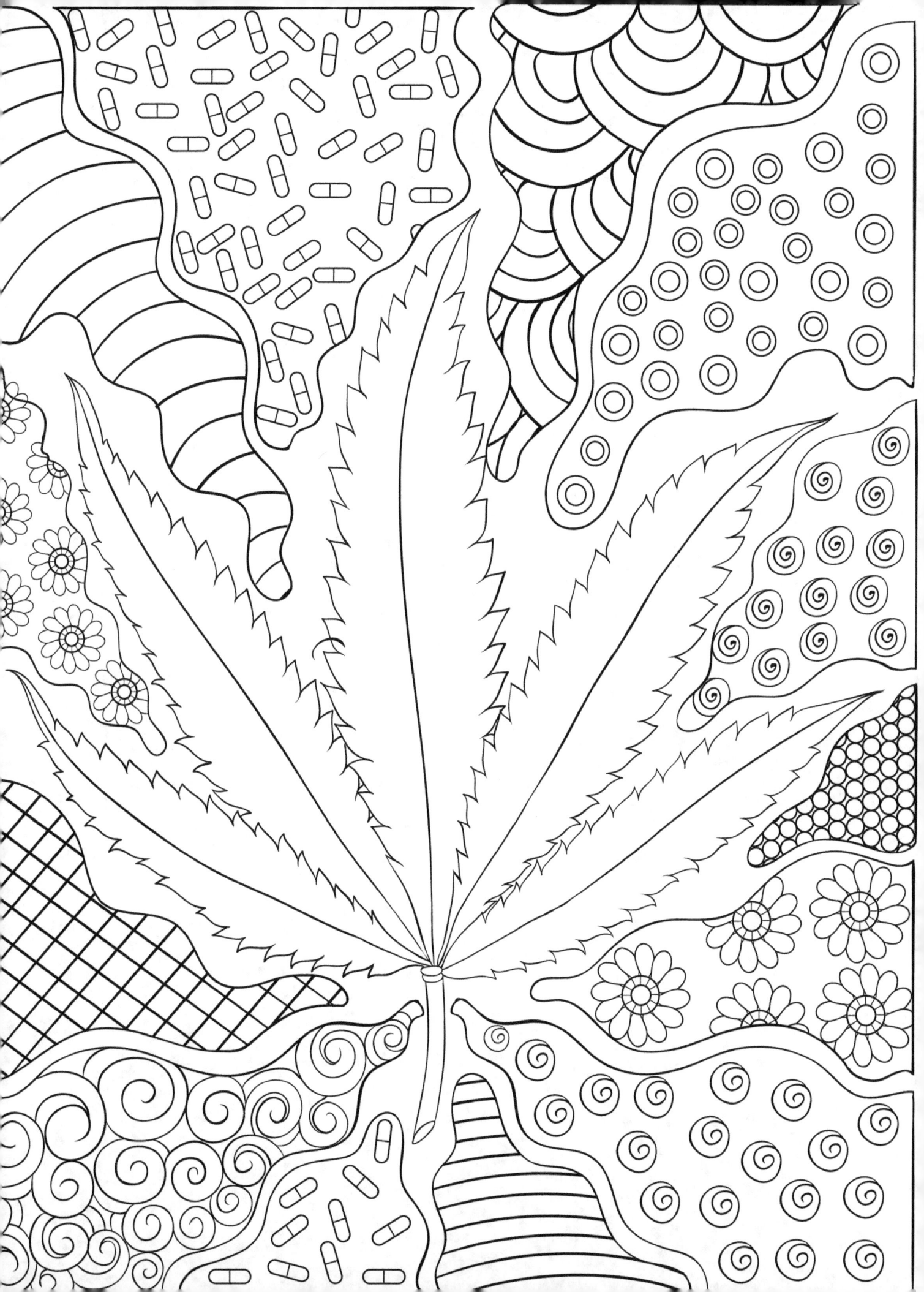

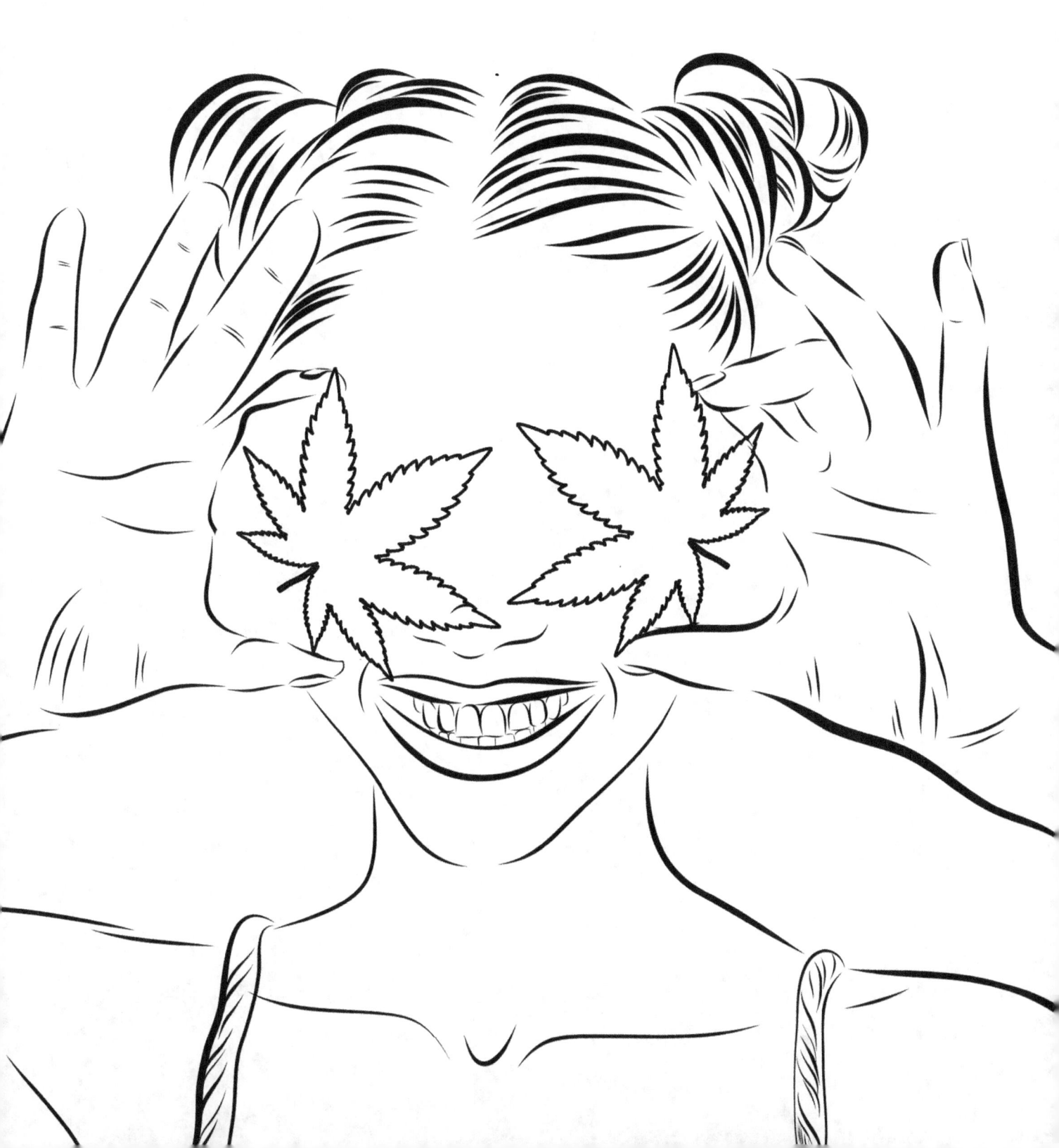

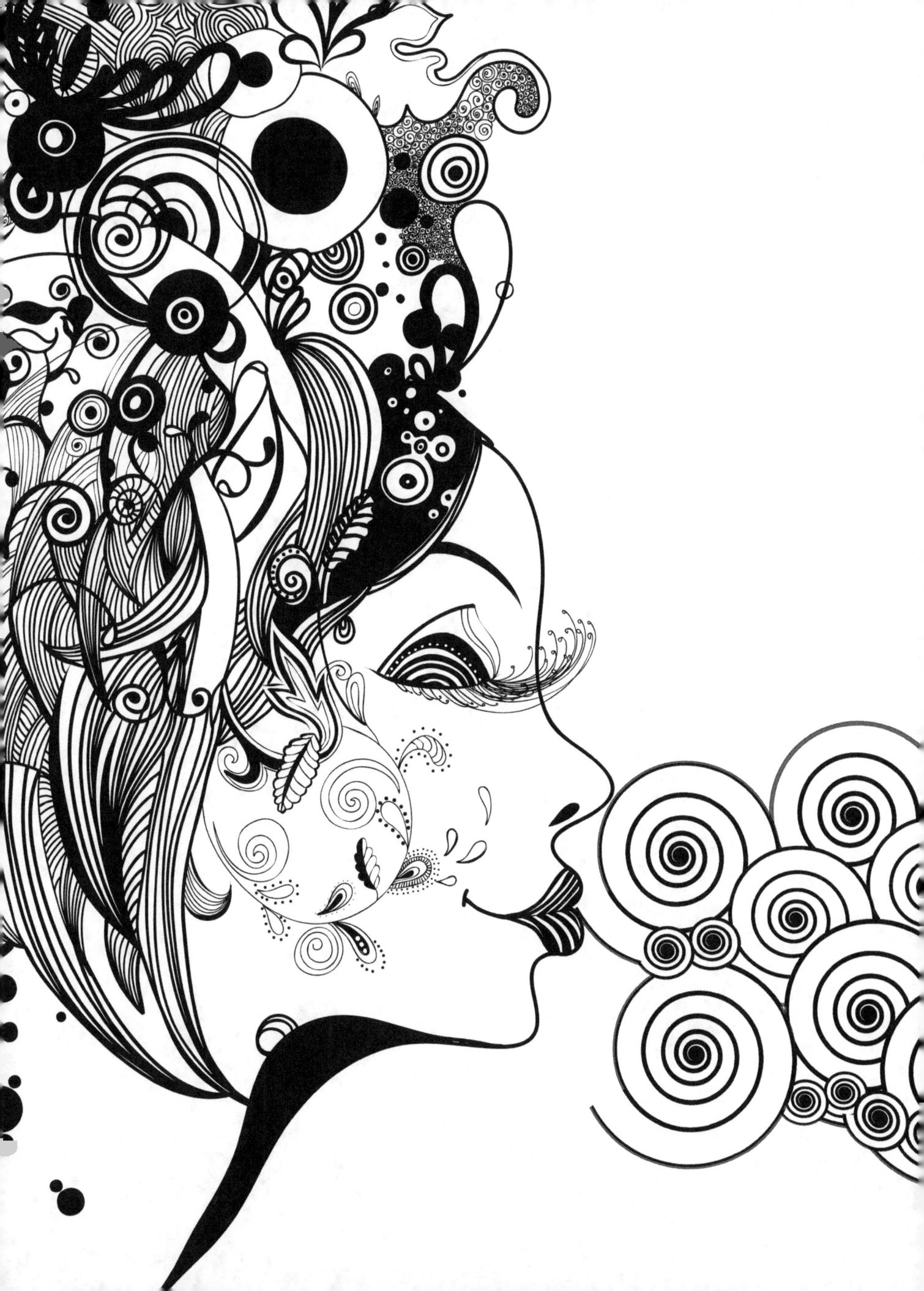

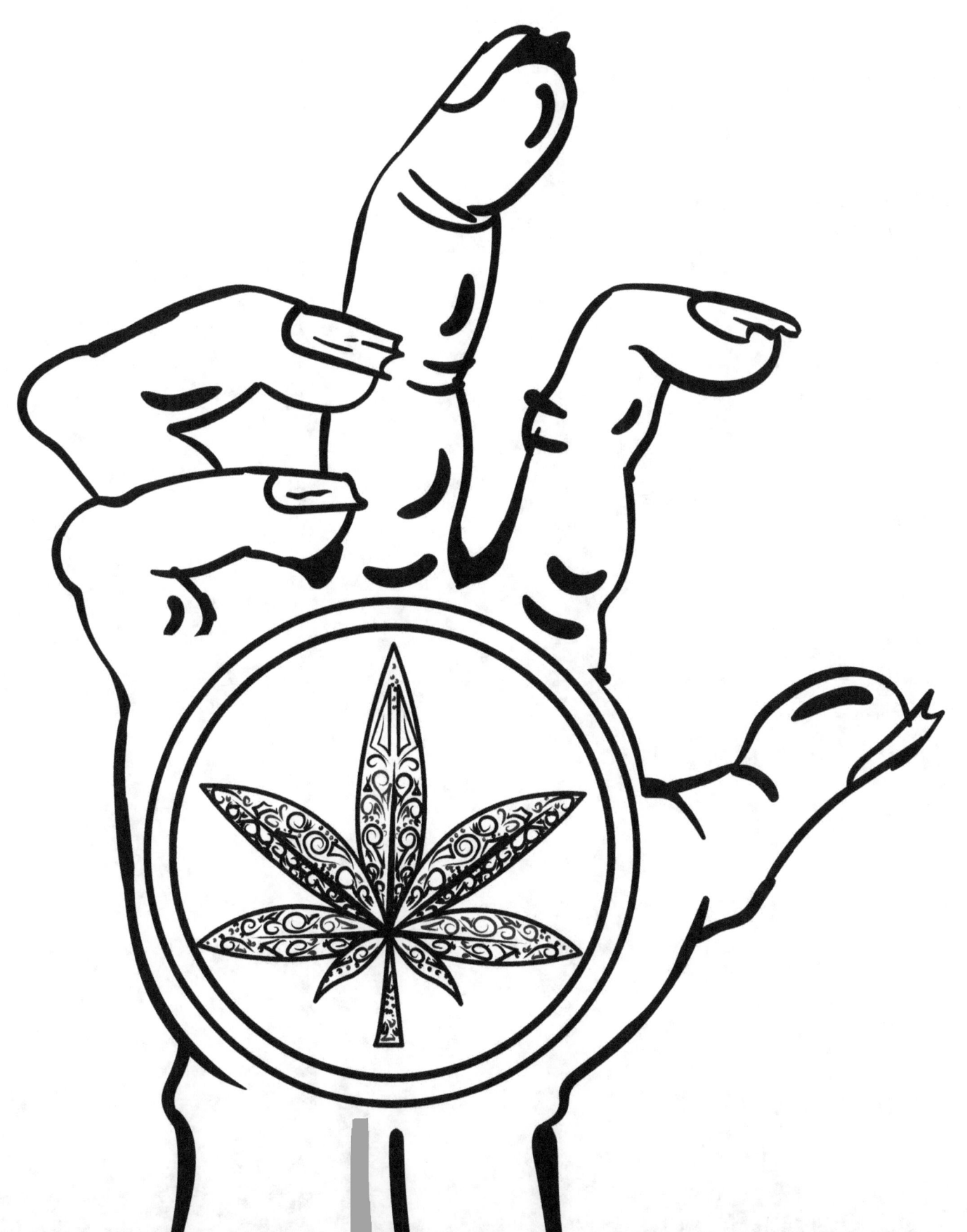

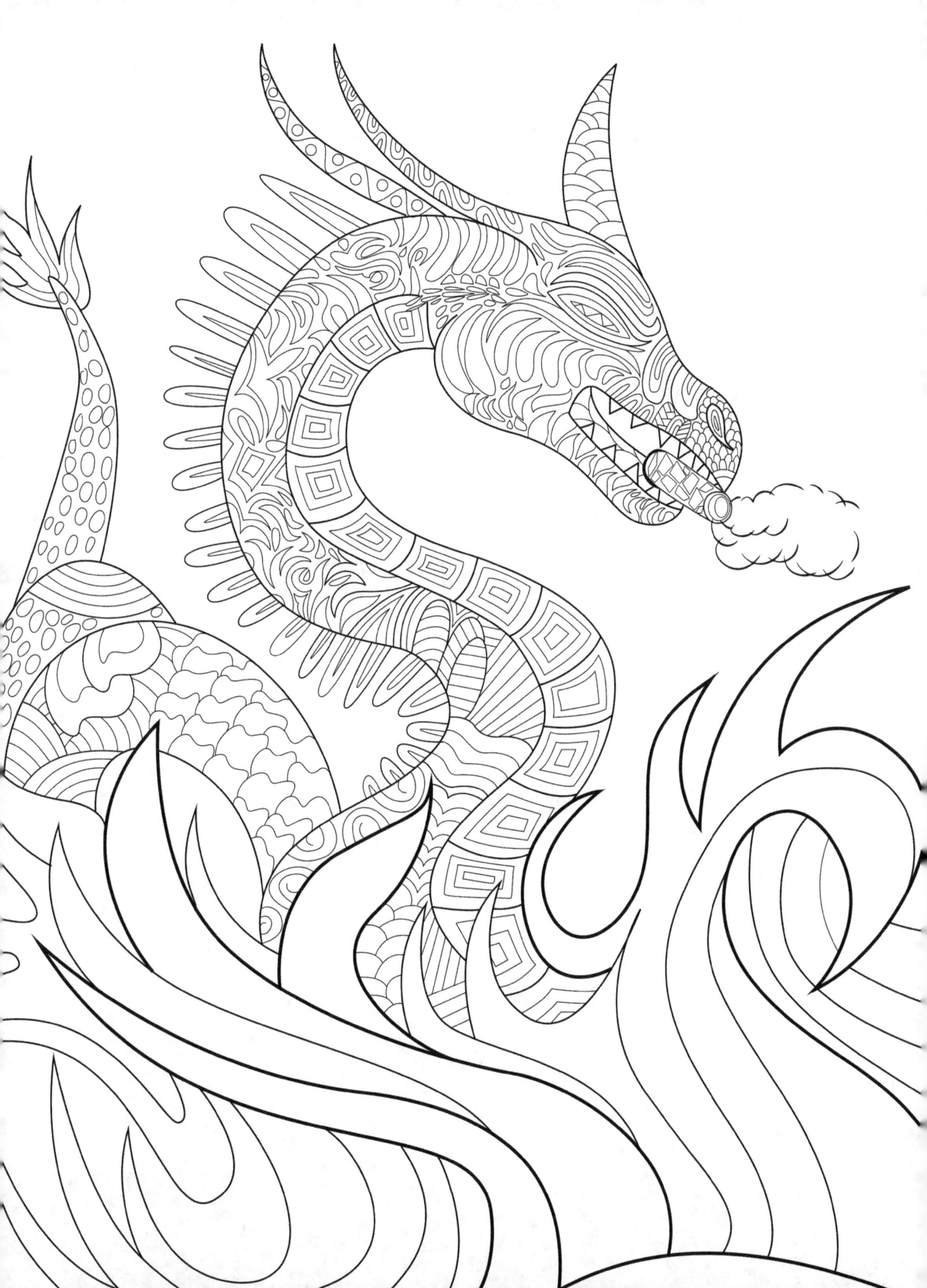

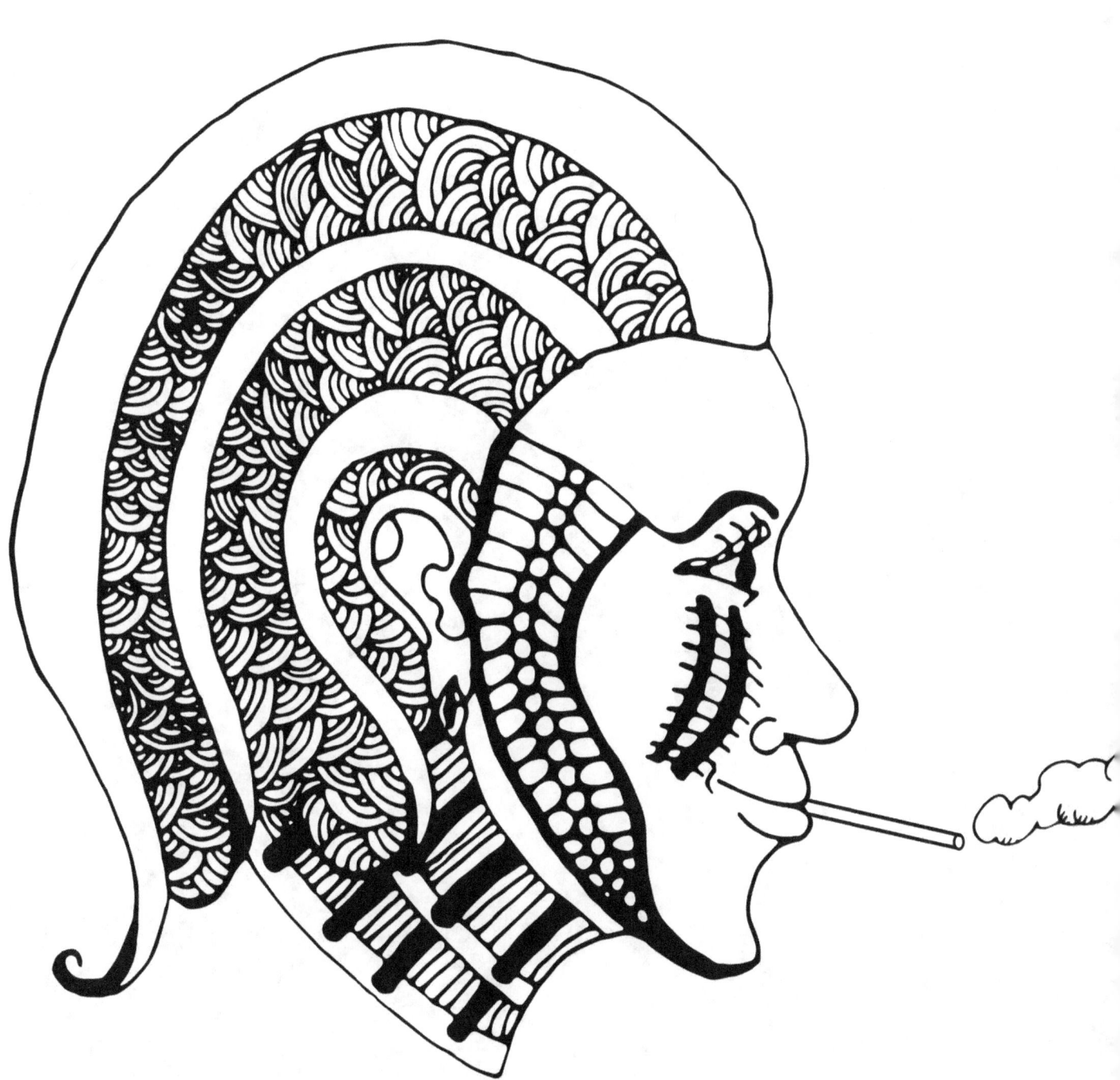

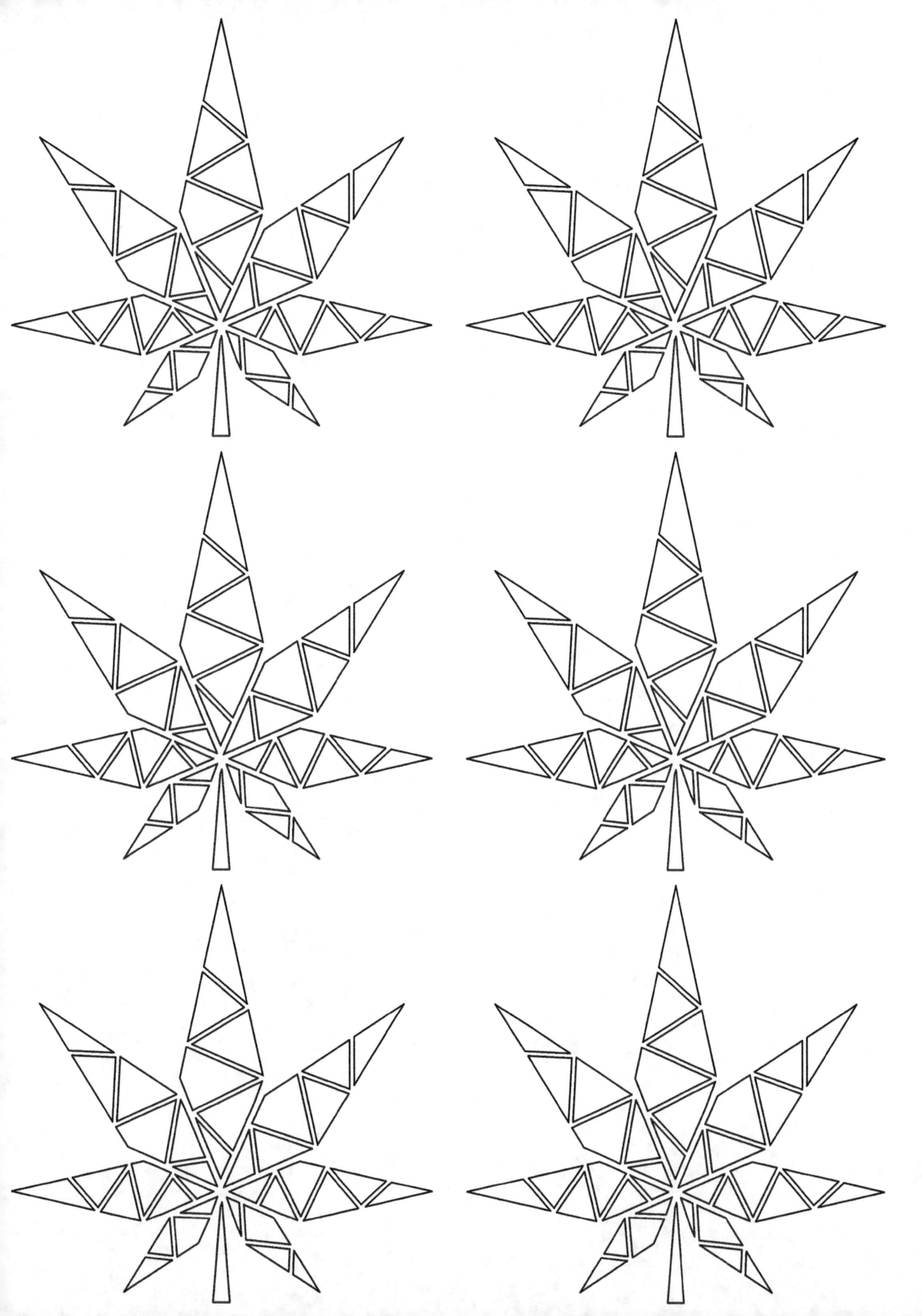

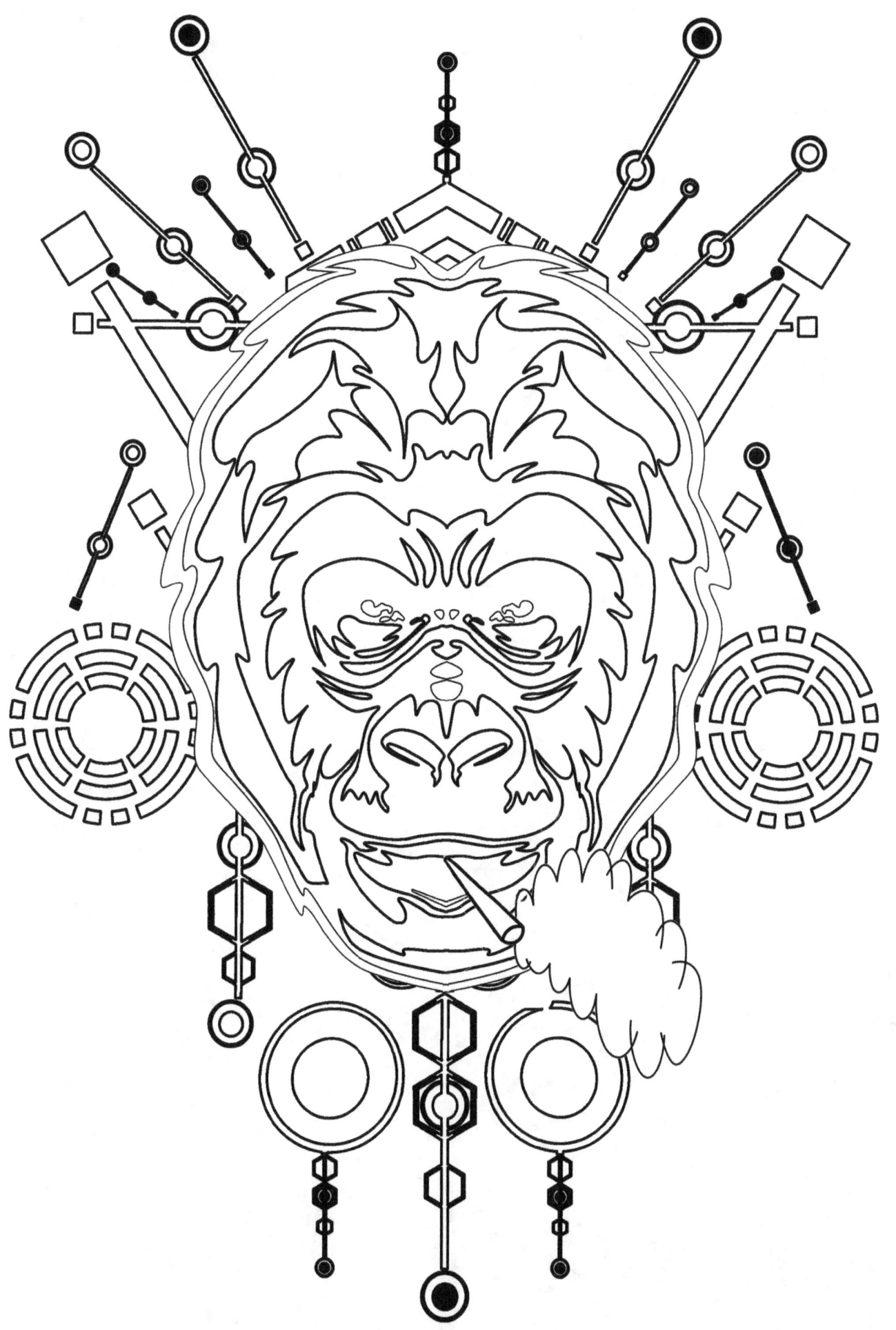

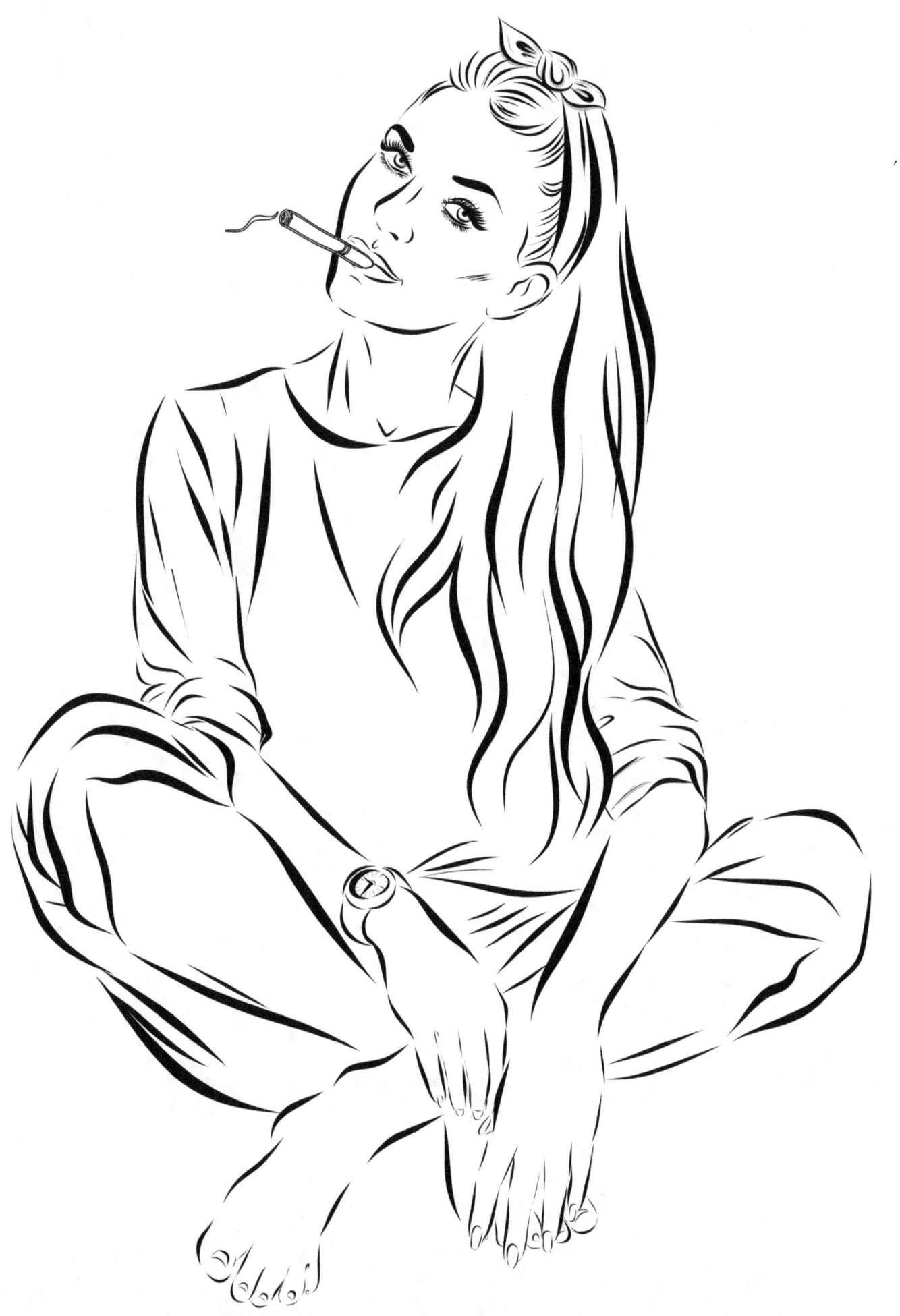

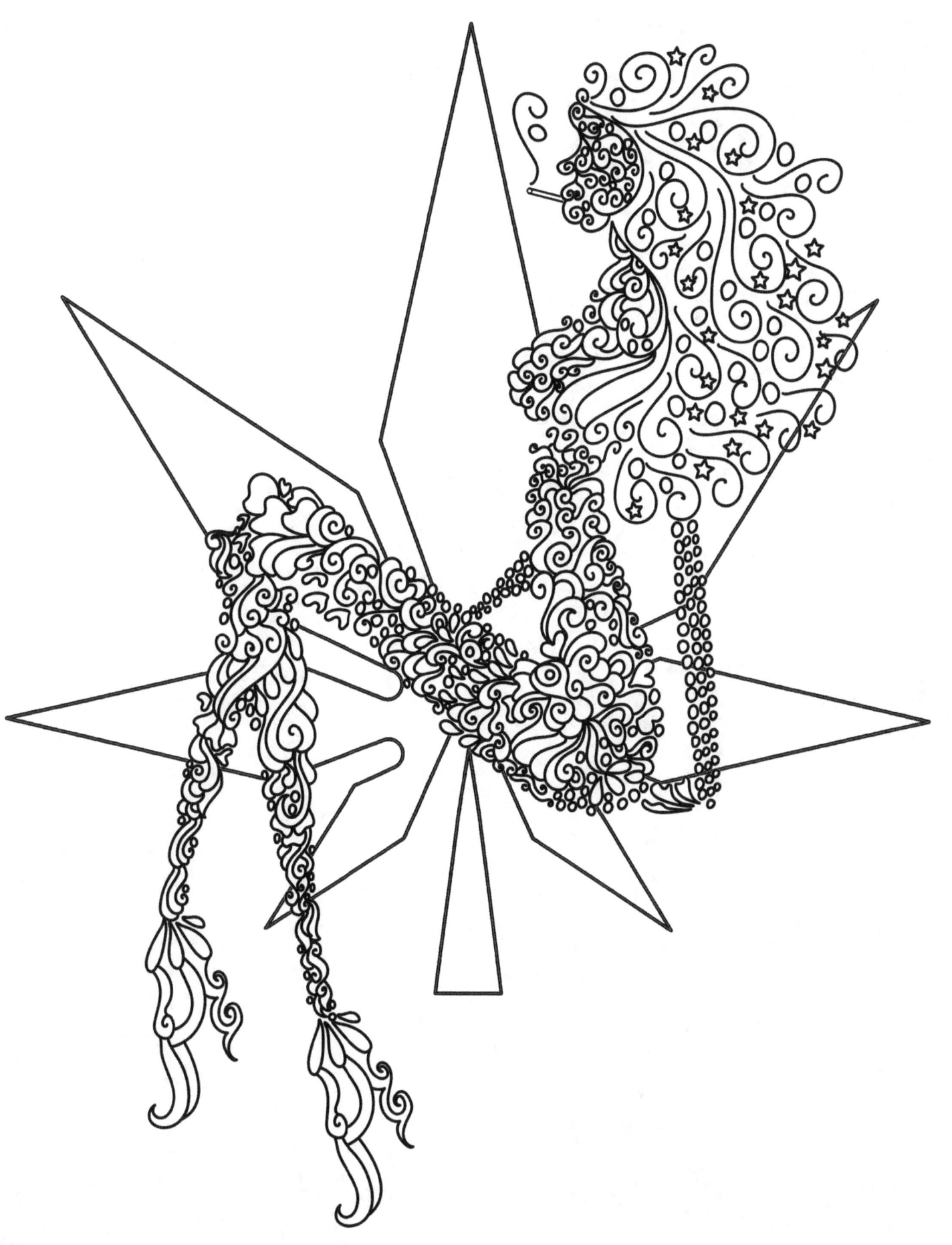

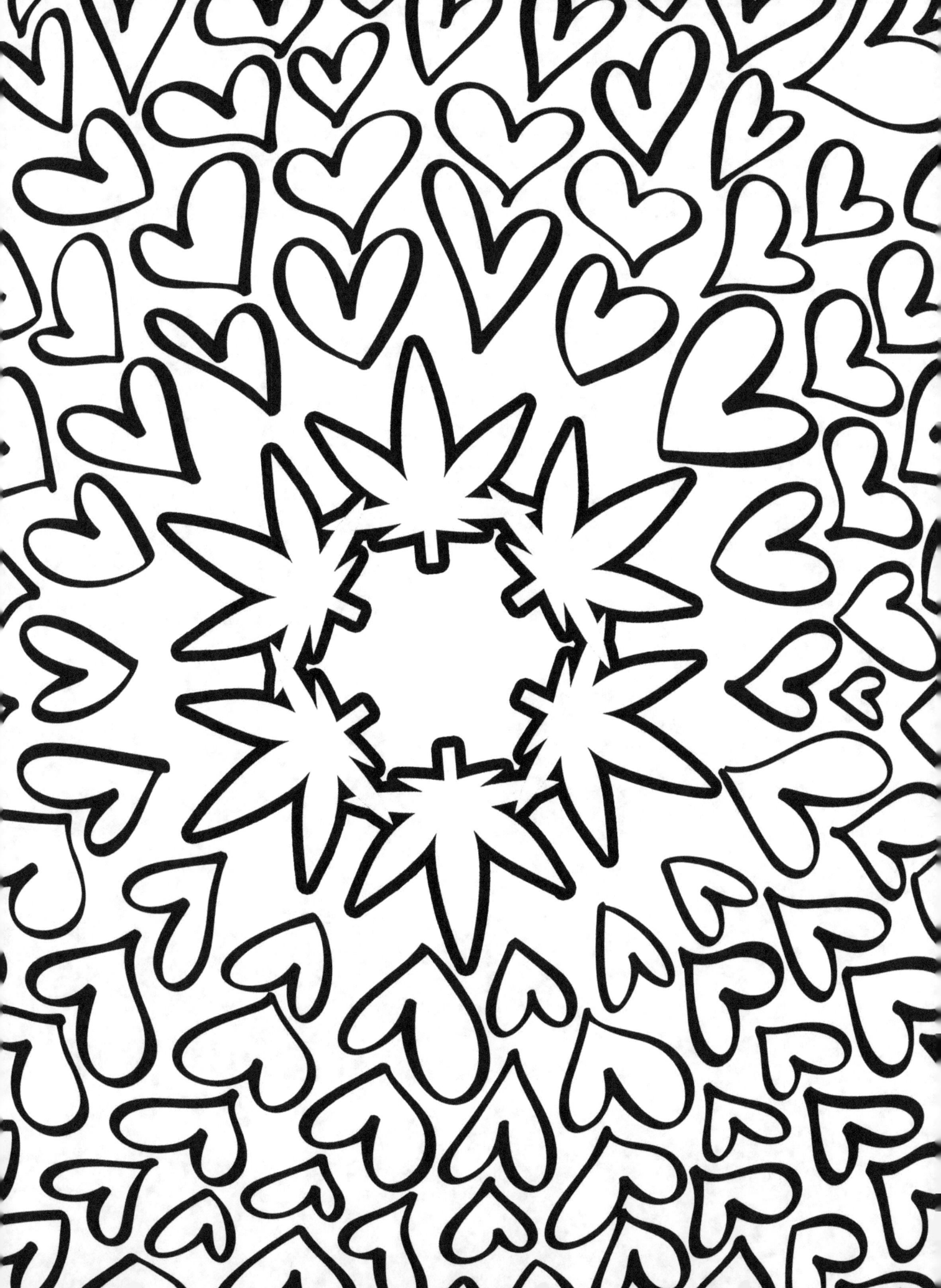

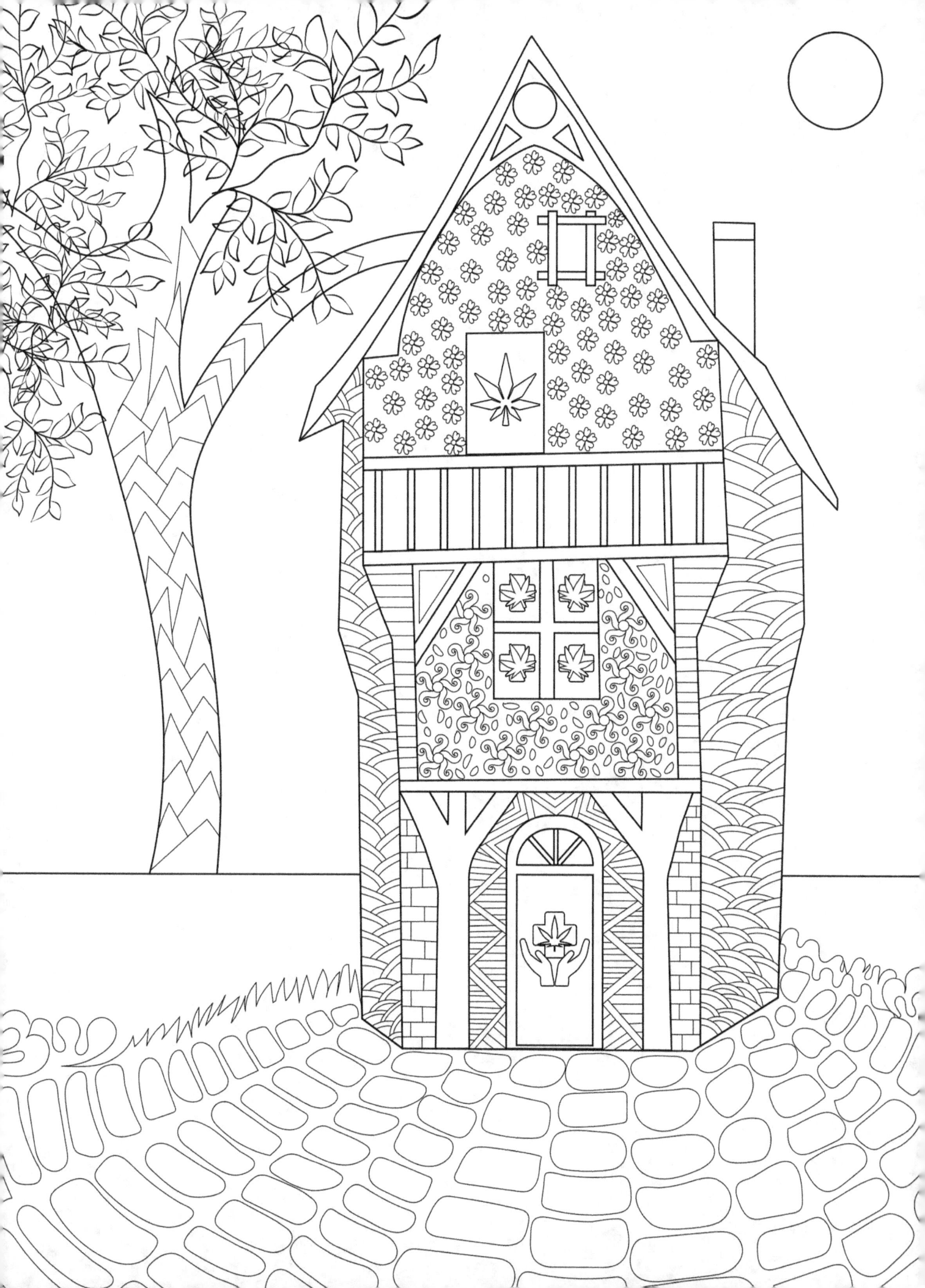

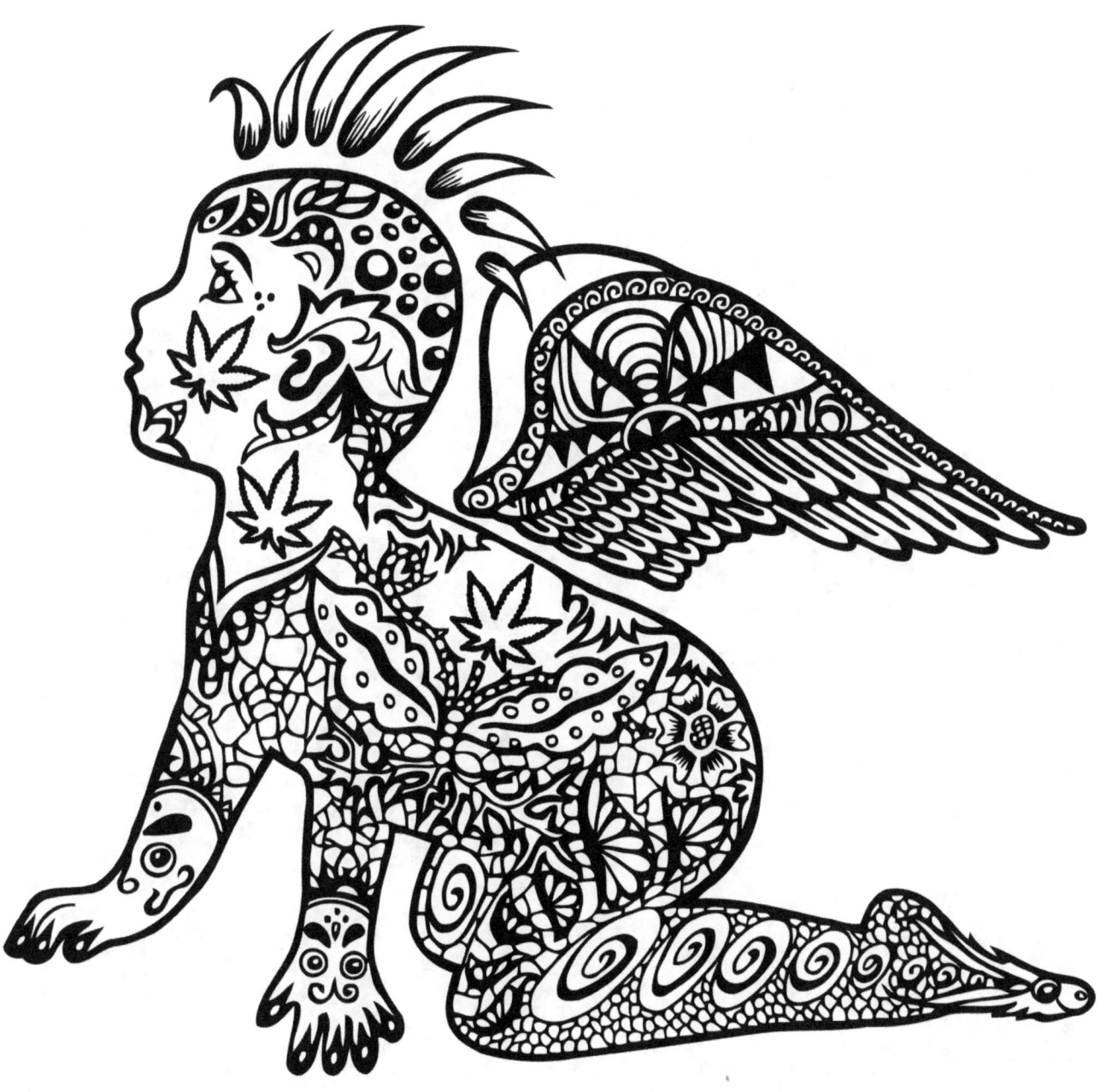

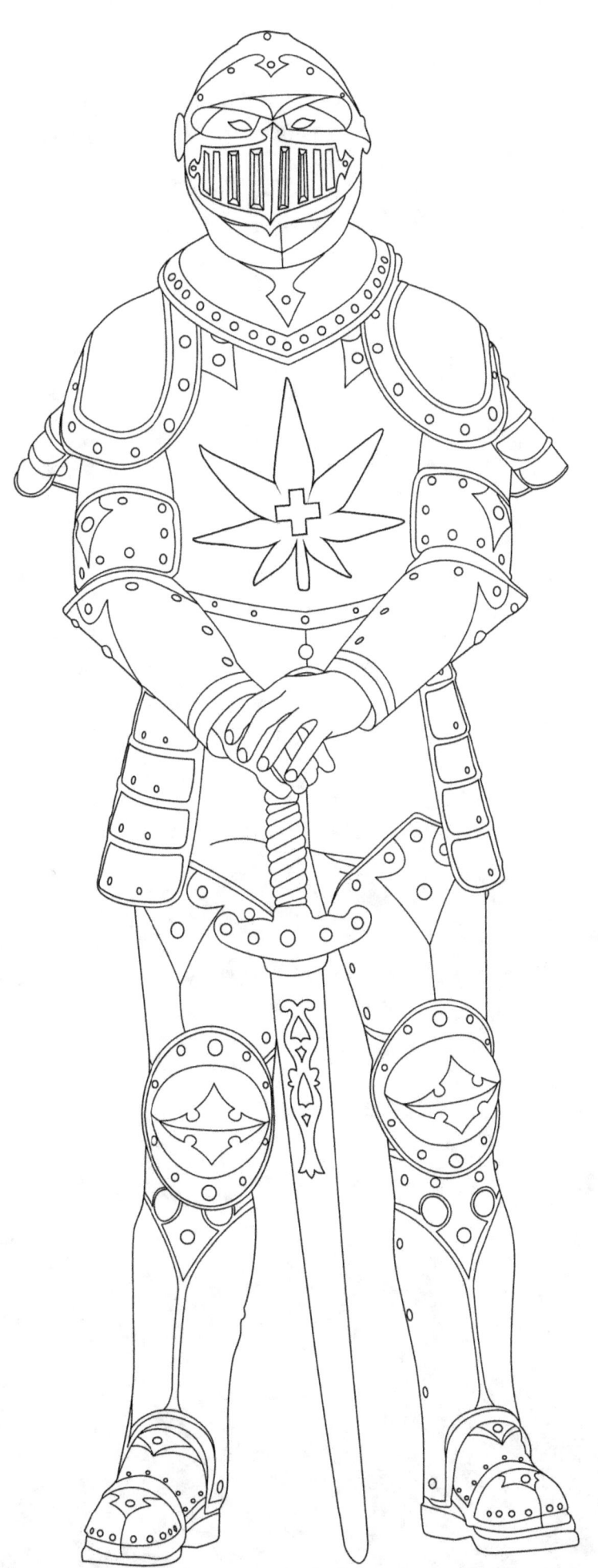

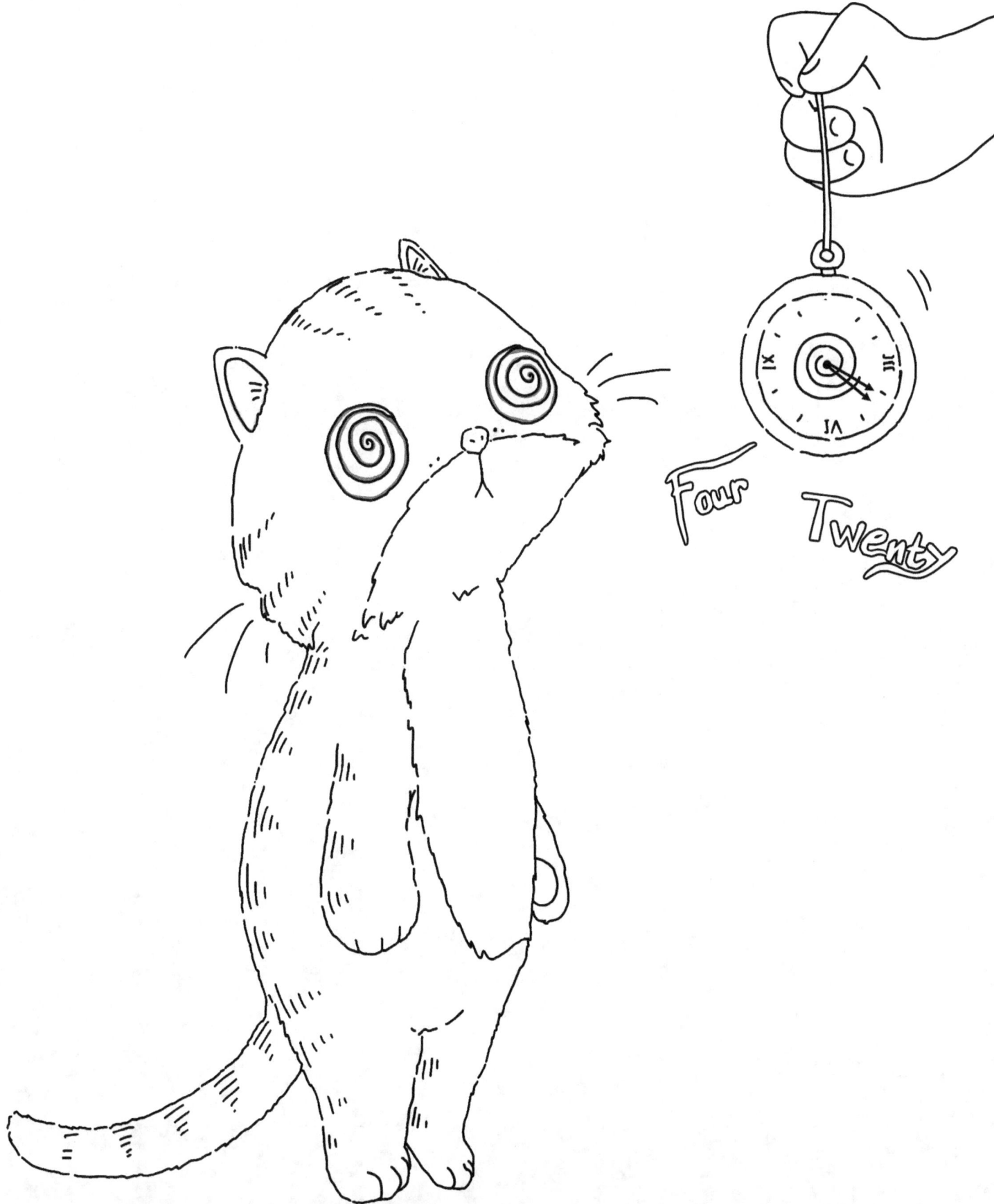

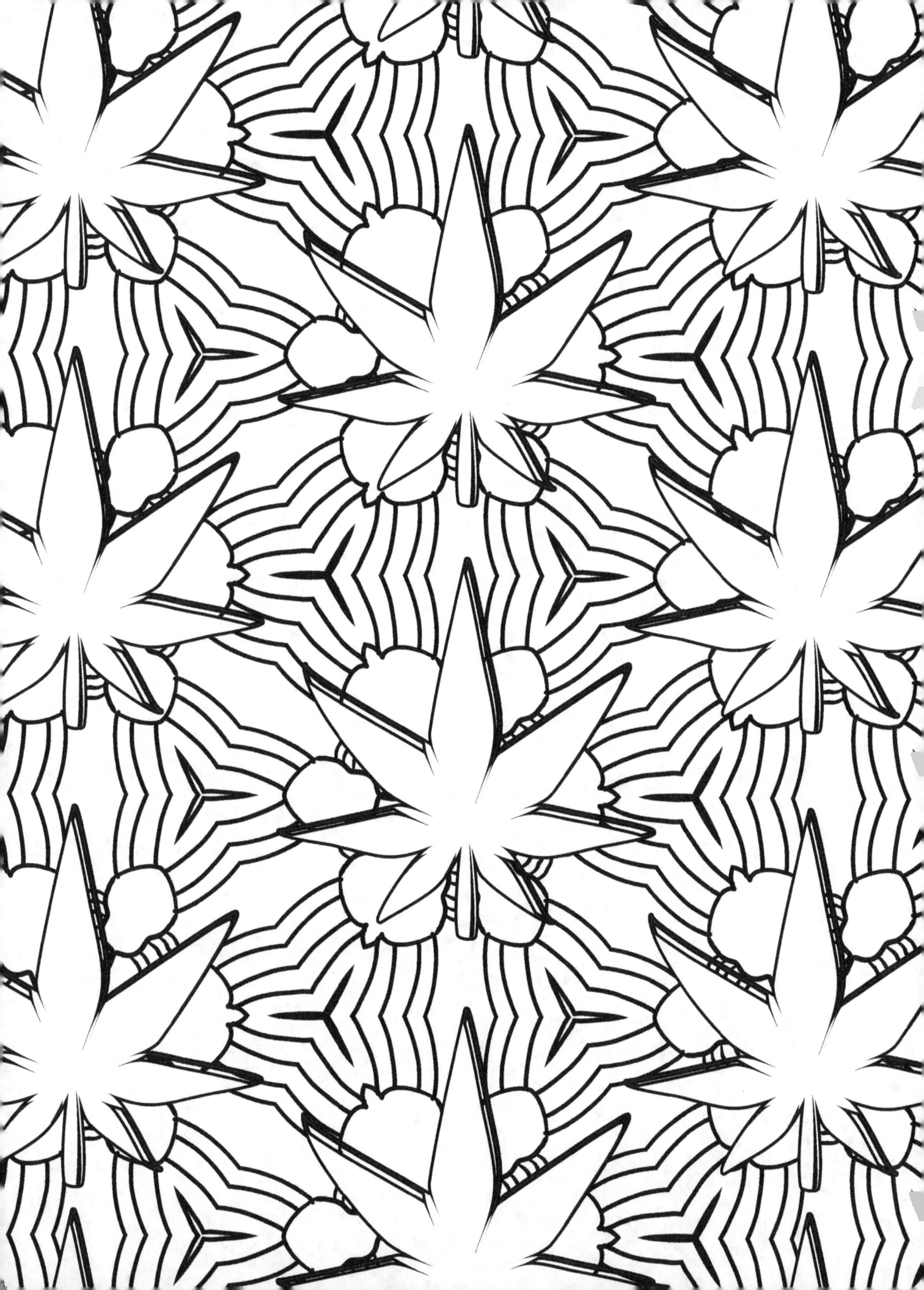

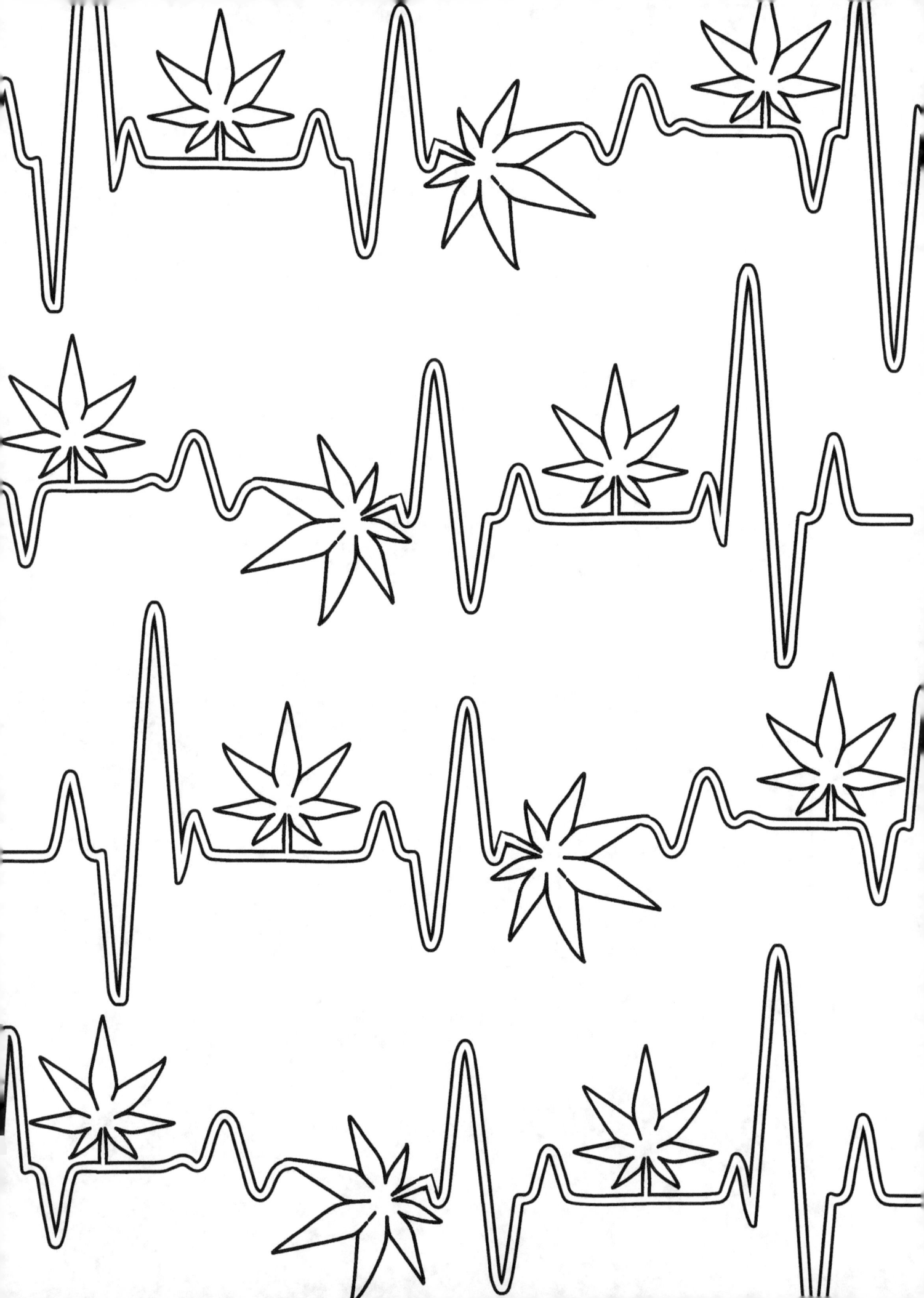

Color Test Page

More Fresh Baked
Marijuana Coloring Fun!

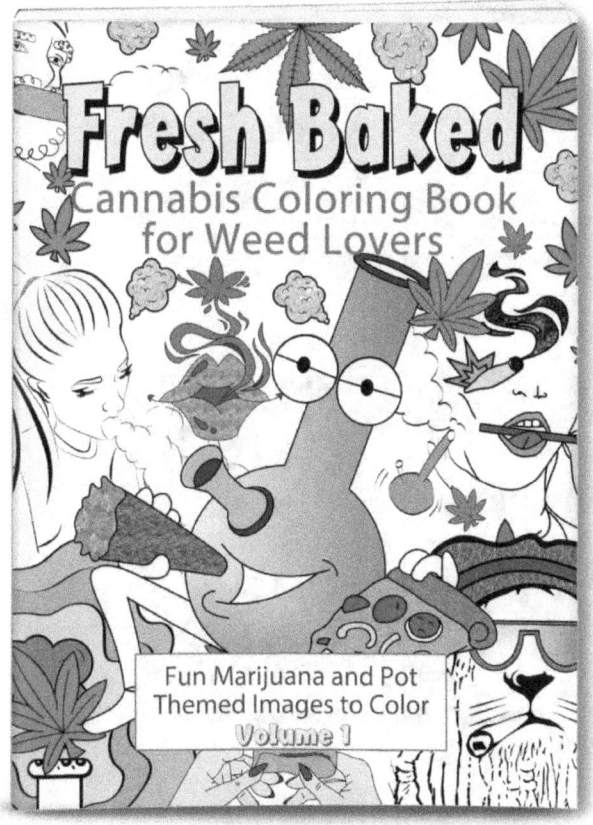

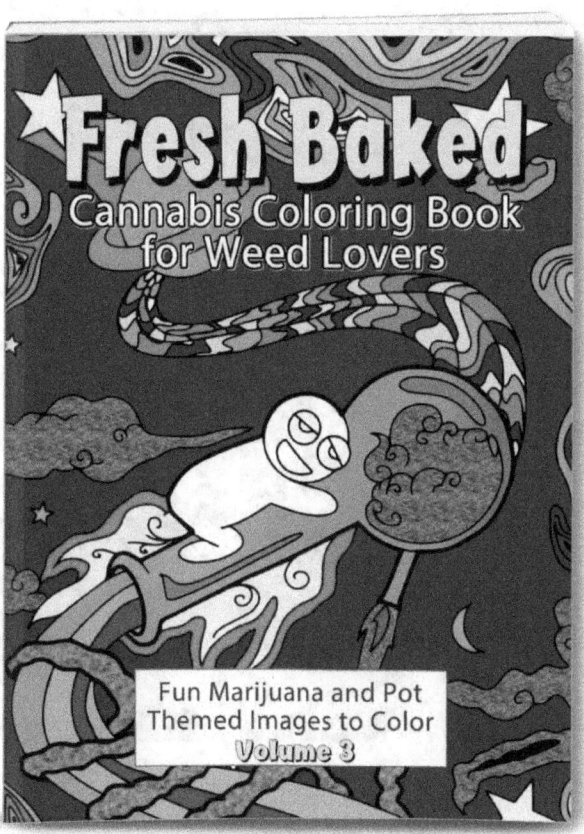

Amazon: 194767613X

ISBN: 978-1947676138

Amazon: 1947676156

ISBN: 978-1947676152

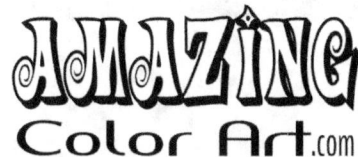

Enjoy these great titles and more by Amazing Color Art!

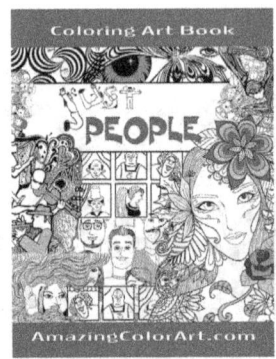

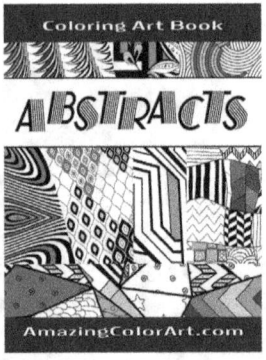

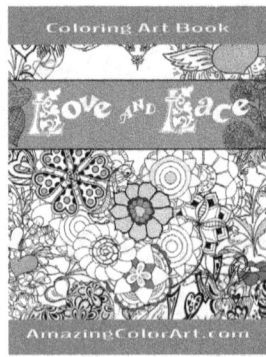

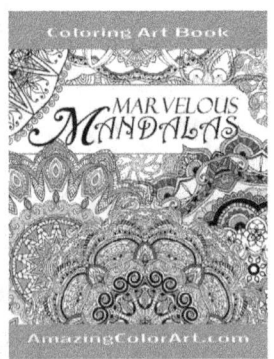

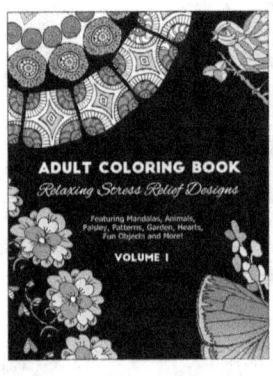

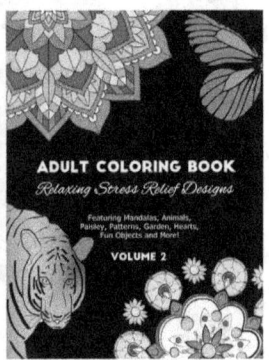

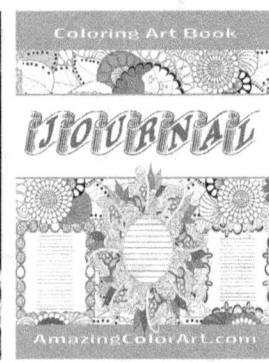

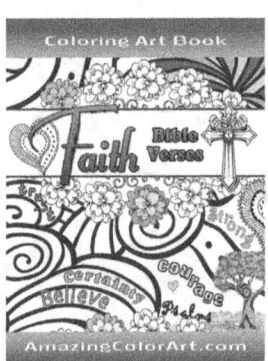

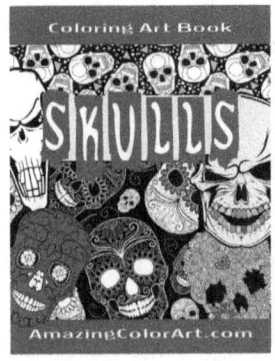

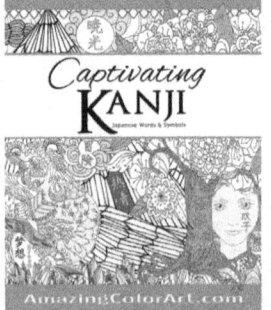

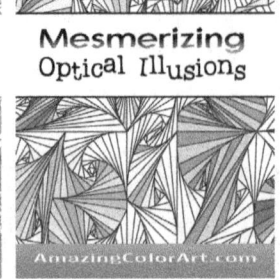

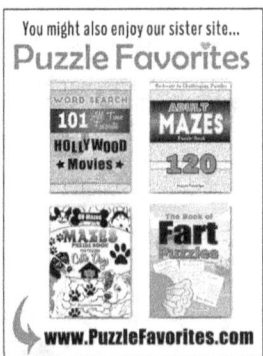

www.ingramcontent.com/pod-product-compliance
Lightning Source LLC
Chambersburg PA
CBHW081611220526
45468CB00010B/2842